Mobile Web Development

Building mobile websites, SMS and MMS messaging,
mobile payments, and automated voice call systems
with XHTML MP, WCSS, and mobile AJAX

Nirav Mehta

BIRMINGHAM - MUMBAI

Mobile Web Development

First published: February 2008

Production Reference: 1300108

Published by Packt Publishing Ltd.
32 Lincoln Road
Olton
Birmingham, B27 6PA, UK.

ISBN 978-1-847193-43-8

www.packtpub.com

Cover Image by Bharath Kumar (bharath.rbk@gmail.com)

Credits

Author

Nirav Mehta

Reviewer

Michael Peacock

Senior Acquisition Editor

David Barnes

Development Editor

Nikhil Bangera

Technical Editor

Ajay Shanker

Editorial Manager

Mithil Kulkarni

Project Manager

Abhijeet Deobhakta

Project Coordinators

Snehal Raut

Zenab Kapasi

Indexer

Hemangini Bari

Proofreader

Chris Smith

Production Coordinators

Aparna Bhagat

Shantanu Zagade

Cover Work

Aparna Bhagat

About the Author

Nirav Mehta is renowned for his entrepreneurial ventures, his breakthrough ideas, and his contribution to open source. Nirav leads a software development company—Magnet Technologies—from India that specializes in Rich Internet Applications, Web, and Mobile. Nirav believes in simplifying the most complicated ideas and presenting them in lucid language.

Over the last ten years, Nirav has written and spoken on a variety of topics. He has also been instrumental in localization efforts in India and training programmers to be effective developers. He blogs at www.mehtanirav.com.

My love and thanks to my parents. It's your support and freedom that lets me do all things I love! Thank you!

I would like to thank Mayank Sharma, for his recommendations. Without you, the book wouldn't be possible.

Thanks to David Barnes, Packt's Acquisition Editor. Your comments, guidance, and blog have inspired me a lot.

I would like to thank Micheal Peacock and the team at Packt—Nikhil Bangera, Patricia Weir, Snehal Raut, Ajay Shanker, Sagara Naik, and everyone else. You guys are amazing! I will always remember how hard you worked to get the book out near my wedding, and the superb suggestions throughout.

Of course, the team at Magnet! Ashok, Vishal, and Harshad—you have been with me in all the ups and downs, I cherish your partnership. All Magneteers, thank you for being a great team!

I also appreciate the readers of this book! I believe you are up to something big, and hope my work helps you achieve it.

And finally, my wonderful wife, Nikita. I stole time from you for the book. Thanks for your constant love, encouragement, and reminders!

About the Reviewer

Michael Peacock is a web developer and senior partner of Peacock, Carter & Associates (`http://www.peacockcarter.co.uk`) a web design and development business. Michael loves building websites and web applications, and when he isn't, likes to read, watch films, and occasionally take part in amateur dramatics.

Table of Contents

Preface

As more users access the Web from their phones and other handhelds, web developers need to learn techniques for targeting these new devices. Sites such as Twitter, Facebook, and Google target mobiles with their services and products. Companies use mobile services to provide staff access to their applications while away from a computer.

This book is a complete, practical guide to writing mobile websites and applications. You will learn how to create mobile-friendly websites, adapt your content to the capabilities of different devices, save bandwidth with compression, and create server-side logic that integrates with a mobile front end. You will also see other methods for integrating your web application with mobile technology: sending and receiving MMS and SMS messages, accepting mobile payments, and working with voice calls to provide spoken interaction.

The book illustrates every technique with practical examples, showing how to use these development methods in the real world. Along the way we show how an example pizza delivery business can use these methods to open up to the mobile web.

Whether you want to provide customers and users of your public website with new ways to access your services, or build applications so that staff can stay up to date while on the road, this book will show you all you need to build a powerful mobile presence.

What This Book Covers

Chapter 1 introduces the Mobile Web and we'll see why mobile web is the next big thing.

Chapter 2 is our first look at the example site we'll be building in the book: "Pizza on the Run" (POTR). Specifically, we look at: picking the best method to deliver your site to mobile browsers, designing navigation and information architecture, setting up a development environment, learning XHTML Mobile Profile—the presentation language for mobile applications, and developing Pizza On The Run's mobile site homepage.

Chapter 3 looks at: designing layouts for the mobile web, using Wireless CSS in design, being aware of differences in mobile browsers, creating the database and code architecture for our example site (POTR), using forms on the mobile web, handling user authentication, testing our work in simulators, constraining user input with Wireless CSS, and applying special effects using Wireless CSS.

Chapter 4 covers: understanding the Lowest Common Denominator method, finding and comparing features of different mobile devices, deciding to adapt or not, adapting and progressively enhancing the POTR application using Wireless Abstraction Library, detecting device capabilities, evaluating tools that can aid in adaptation, and moving your blog to mobile.

Chapter 5 specifically looks at: running a ready.mobi test on your site, creating the structure, design, markup, and navigation for best user experience, and collecting user behavior data to keep enhancing the site.

Chapter 6 looks at sending text messages, and in the process covers the fundamentals of using third-party services for messaging. We specifically take a look at: updating order status for POTR, selecting an SMS gateway provider and setting up an account, sending text messages using the gateway's API, understanding how an SMS message is delivered, getting delivery status updates, setting up our own SMS gateway, and sending bulk messages.

Chapter 7 covers: creating Multimedia Messages for special offers at POTR, controlling message presentation, sending Multimedia Messages through our gateway, and receiving photos from customers via MMS.

Chapter 8 explores and set up a mobile payment system for POTR. Specifically, we look at: getting money through PayPal, evaluating mobile payment methods—their pros and cons, security concerns in mobile payments, using SMS in mobile payment, Premium SMS and Short Codes, and receiving Text Messages via a short code.

Chapter 9 looks at: setting up an interactive voice response platform, playing pre-recorded audio and text to speech, accepting keypad inputs, accepting voice input and doing speech recognition, performing dynamic calculations on input, and integrating with server-side scripting.

Chapter 10 covers how to use AJAX on mobile platforms. We specifically look at: getting pizza recipes via AJAX, enabling AJAX in forms, understanding iPhone application development, and more about building rich mobile apps.

Chapter 11 looks at: trends in mobile web applications, mobile widgets and developments of the browser, connectivity — mobile networks, occasionally connected devices, open Handset Alliance and Google's Android system, and resources to keep abreast of the mobile scene.

What You Need for This Book

You do not need any specific software/hardware to benefit from the book. But:

- To run the examples, you will need a PHP/MySQL setup.
- You will need a Windows system to install mobile emulators and IVR software.

Conventions

In this book, you will find a number of styles of text that distinguish between different kinds of information. Here are some examples of these styles, and an explanation of their meaning.

There are three styles for code. Code words in text are shown as follows: "We can include other contexts through the use of the `include` directive."

A block of code will be set as follows:

```
CREATE TABLE `trackingdata` (
  `id` int(10) unsigned NOT NULL auto_increment,
  `userId` int(10) unsigned NOT NULL,
  `sessionId` varchar(40)  NOT NULL,
```

When we wish to draw your attention to a particular part of a code block, the relevant lines or items will be made bold:

```
'".getenv('HTTP_REFERER')."', '".getenv('HTTP_USER_AGENT')."',
'".serialize($_REQUEST)."')";
  $GLOBALS['db']->Query($query);
  $_SESSION['tdId'] = $GLOBALS['db']->GetCurrentId();
```

New terms and important words are introduced in a bold-type font. Words that you see on the screen, in menus or dialog boxes for example, appear in our text like this: "clicking the Next button moves you to the next screen".

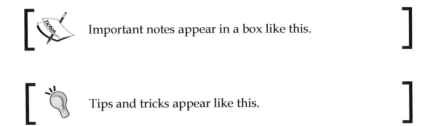

Important notes appear in a box like this.

Tips and tricks appear like this.

Reader Feedback

Feedback from our readers is always welcome. Let us know what you think about this book, what you liked or may have disliked. Reader feedback is important for us to develop titles that you really get the most out of.

To send us general feedback, simply drop an email to feedback@packtpub.com, making sure to mention the book title in the subject of your message.

If there is a book that you need and would like to see us publish, please send us a note in the SUGGEST A TITLE form on www.packtpub.com or email suggest@packtpub.com.

If there is a topic that you have expertise in and you are interested in either writing or contributing to a book, see our author guide on www.packtpub.com/authors.

Customer Support

Now that you are the proud owner of a Packt book, we have a number of things to help you to get the most from your purchase.

Downloading the Example Code for the Book

Visit http://www.packtpub.com/support, and select this book from the list of titles to download any example code or extra resources for this book. The files available for download will then be displayed.

The downloadable files contain instructions on how to use them.

Errata

Although we have taken every care to ensure the accuracy of our contents, mistakes do happen. If you find a mistake in one of our books—maybe a mistake in text or code—we would be grateful if you would report this to us. By doing this you can save other readers from frustration, and help to improve subsequent versions of this book. If you find any errata, report them by visiting http://www.packtpub.com/support, selecting your book, clicking on the **Submit Errata** link, and entering the details of your errata. Once your errata are verified, your submission will be accepted and the errata added to the list of existing errata. The existing errata can be viewed by selecting your title from http://www.packtpub.com/support.

Questions

You can contact us at questions@packtpub.com if you are having a problem with some aspect of the book, and we will do our best to address it.

This book is dedicated to
my parents – Vinod & Nayna
and my wife – Nikita;
for their love and support

1
Getting Mobile

When Evan Williams, founder of Blogger and Odeo, had to pick up what he would do next to revolutionize the Web, he decided to go mobile. Evan returned the VC money to focus on Twitter—a service that allows keeping in touch with friends via alerts to and from your mobile phone (and instant messenger and web)! After six months of launch, Twitter had reached 50,000 active users. The number doubled to 100,000 in just one month after Twitter won the Best Blog award at South By South West conference.

Evan mentioned "Best Blog" was a weird category for Twitter, as Twitter is not a blog. But Twitter's growth has been phenomenal. As Ewan Spence of The Podcast Network puts it, "Twitter has got Americans texting!" And that included a US Presidential candidate!

The way it works is very simple. Whenever you want to update your friends about what you are doing, just pick up your phone, type an SMS, and send it to a special shortcode number. Twitter broadcasts it to all your friends and posts it on your Twitter page. Your friends will know what you are up to, whether they are online or on the move.

If you have a lot of friends, you may love getting text messages about what they are eating and what their cat is doing. Or you may hate the SMS beeps at all odd hours. But it is a fact that Twitter is a big-time success. And it shows where things are moving.

Things are moving mobile!

Broadtexter allows music bands to broadcast messages to their fans via SMS. With a Broadtexter account, the band get a simple widget they can place on their site. Fans register using this widget. When the band are doing a show, they go to Broadtexter, select the area of the show, and send out an SMS broadcast to all those fans with the venue and time of the show. Unlike the conventional thinking that people would not like such updates, the idea has been a hit. Many bands had people coming in and thanking them for the SMS! They weren't doing anything else that evening, and the last minute text message excited them to get to the show. The band not only sold more tickets but also got a new way to keep in touch with fans.

Imagine Twitter or Broadtexter without the mobile connectivity. We will not go to a friend's blog to read short updates on what she or he is doing. We will forget the reminder a band had emailed two days ago about today's event. Twitter and Broadtexter are successful primarily because they allow updates over mobile devices in a quick and convenient manner.

And it is not only text messages. Google has a full blown mobile site. You can access it using a mobile phone or a PDA, and perform a search just like you would do from a desktop. You can navigate the results using the limited keyboard you have on the device and still get the job done.

Web applications are now reaching where their users are. Not just in front of their desktop, but also when they are traveling, or when they are driving looking for a good restaurant in the neighborhood.

Welcome to the world of Mobile Web!

What is Mobile Web?

Simply put, mobile web refers to the Web being accessed from mobile devices like cell phones and PDAs. The reach and capabilities of mobile devices has grown phenomenally over the last three years. Almost all mobile phones now can access the Internet in some or the other way. All PDAs have a tiny web browser built in. People are getting used to accessing information from the Web over their phones. Many use PDAs to check their emails and manage other bits of information. Early adopters of technology have already been blogging from their mobiles and viewing online photos and videos while they are traveling. Mobile web is all of that. Any website accessed from a mobile device is mobile web—whether it's been tailored to work on a mobile or not!

Mobile Web Integration is Connecting the Two!

We use mobile phones mainly to communicate with people—either voice or text. PDAs so far have been used for managing schedules and contacts, apart from some occasional office productivity work and games! The Web on the other hand has evolved greatly over the years. From the early days of simple HTML markup linking a few pages, to the Web 2.0 collaborative ecosystem, things have matured a lot. If you come to think of it, we can't expect a world without the Web or mobile devices today!

You may have done a lot of web programming and might be wondering how you can develop for mobile devices. Or you may want to add mobile features to your existing site. This book will teach you all that. Reading through the book, you can port your website to mobile devices. You can AJAXify your mobile site and integrate SMS or MMS messaging. You will even be able to accept payments via mobile and use intelligent interactive voice-response systems. With this book, you can bring web applications to mobile devices, integrating them with mobile-specific features!

By the way, we are not going to talk about mobile application development. We are not even going to talk about web application development. You don't need any J2ME knowledge or C++. All we assume is that you have a basic knowledge of HTML and some server-side programming technology. We will use PHP for the examples in the book, but you can easily customize them to any other language. We will explain different mobile technologies, so it's alright if you don't know them already!

The First Step—Understanding Mobile Devices

Go to any electronics store, and you will have hundreds of mobile phones to choose from. The shelf life of a mobile phone model is less than 18 months now. People change their phones every two years, and companies push new models every month. Mobile phones are not the only mobile devices! With pocket-sized computing devices—PDAs, micro notebooks, and even handheld notebooks—the options are bewildering. We will include both mobile phones and pocket-sized devices whenever we refer to mobile devices. Let us discuss some specific features and limitations of these mobile devices.

Mobile Phones

Mobile phones are the largest segment of mobile devices. Mobile phones typically come in "candy bar", "sliding box", or "clam shell" form. You surely have seen a variety of them. Mobile phones have a specially designed processor and run some kind of operating system. Symbian and Windows Mobile are widely used operating systems on mobile phones, and many phone manufacturers develop their own systems as well.

The most important use of a mobile phone is to talk. Then, you could use it to take photos, send messages, and play music. In the last three years, mobile phones have seen a number of innovations. All this has resulted in a vast variety of devices in the market—from simple feature phones to smart phones.

Color phones are a norm now, yet there are millions of monochrome devices around. The screen size, resolution, and color density varies greatly. You will see screen sizes from 120x120 to 320x240 and more.

The standard input mechanism for mobile phones is a 12-key pad with additional function keys. Some phones have a joystick that can be used for navigation. Wider-screen models sometimes feature a stylus-based input system or an on-screen keyboard. Phones like the iPhone have touch-sensitive panels, and some have accessories that you can attach to get a full QWERTY keyboard.

Mobile phones come in sizes that fit your pocket—some are incredibly small and some as big as a pencil box. Sleek and slim designs are in vogue—especially because a mobile phone is also a style statement. Having the latest model is a status symbol in many markets!

Referred to as SMS (Short Message Service, Message, or Text depending on the part of the world you are from), these 160 character text messages have revolutionized mobile usage. SMS is now used for all sorts of business and entertainment purposes. MMS (Multimedia Message Service) allows you to send pictures, sounds, and full videos to others just as you send emails.

But if there is one thing that changed mobile phones from communication devices to consumer goods, it is the camera. Starting with VGA quality images (640x480 pixels), today's mobile phones are equipped with five-megapixel cameras, flash, and other tools to add effects to the photographs. Millions have turned into amateur photographers just because of the camera in their phone. The Internet is full of funny and dirty video clips taken from mobile phones.

Not everyone could afford an iPod. So, mobile companies started adding MP3 support to their phones. Use of MP3 ringtones and swapping music files has become a norm. Listening to radio using the phone has shot up too.

And that's not all. As these phones are little computers themselves, you can develop applications that extend their functionality or add new features. Application development over Symbian, J2ME, BREW, or Palm is very popular. Each phone comes with a set of applications and utilities, and there are thousands of developers around the world who develop games and utility applications that run on mobile phones. Google's Android allows you to even replace the built-in applications—giving you full control over your device.

Most of the mobile phones today come with some sort of a web browser. Opera Mini is the most popular browser but there are many more. Different browsers support different features, and break some! Testing across browsers is one of the biggest challenges in mobile web development. The situation is much worse than desktop browsers, and we will see more on this in the coming chapters. The connectivity to the Web depends on the carrier you are on. You may be on GPRS, 3G, Bluetooth, WiFi, or anything in between.

PDAs

Another class of mobile devices is PDAs. Personal Digital Assistants have been around for quite some time and have evolved over this period. They contain many business and productivity applications—email, office productivity, and custom-built software. Typically, they have a QWERTY keyboard—either in the device or onscreen. Phone functionality is an add-on for PDAs, and most consumer PDAs are smart phones now. These handheld devices are merging with phones now, and are very popular with business users.

Other Devices

There are other devices that are used in a mobile fashion. Many embedded devices use mobile technology for communication. Micro notebooks, watches, or cars can be classified here as well. Gaming consoles are also used as web clients these days. We expect many hybrid devices to come up in the next few years leveraging higher computing power and mobile communication technology.

What do people do with all these devices? Understandably, it's much more than voice! Let's see the usage patterns of mobile devices.

Mobile Data Usage is Exploding

Mobiles are used for voice communication generally, but the usage of mobile devices for data communications is growing rapidly. Data usage includes simple things like SMS to mobile web, video and TV on mobile, and other innovations. For mobile companies, this is billions of dollars of additional revenues and for users, these are value-added services. This growth is seen across the globe. Japan, the USA, and China are leading the pack in data usage, but other developed and developing nations are not far behind.

According to a Chetan Sharma's consulting report (`http://www.chetansharma.com/MobilePredictions2008.htm`), Japan and Korea are the benchmarks in terms of mobile data usage, but the USA will soon be the largest revenue-generating market. Brazil, the Netherlands, and Czech regions are already doing more than 30% of their revenues from mobile data. Though a large part of this money is from SMS, other services are gaining larger shares. The USA has 50-60% data revenues from non-SMS services, while Japan and Korea have a higher 70-75%. This trend suggests there is a huge use already of mobile web applications, and it is going to continue not only in these regions but other parts of the world too.

Another interesting thing is that the western European region reports 100% of the population has mobiles—though part of this is due to double phones with single persons and dual reporting. The USA has more than 75% reach. Mobile subscribers around the world have already reached 3 billion, and China and India together are adding close to 13 million every month.

At the same time, the speed of wireless communications is increasing worldwide. Many countries already have 3G and more are gearing up for it. Some are considering 4G and better technologies for faster wireless access. All in all, it means that we can offer services that require faster net access!

Services that were earlier not possible—like video—have already started appearing and will continue to grow. Subscribers set wallpapers, ring tones, ringback tones, true tones, and download full tracks to listen to on their multimedia phones. Most are willing to pay for games. Many companies experimenting (and some betting on) mobile advertising—though 79% of users felt such ads intrusive!

Mobiles are transforming from communication devices to content devices, and will further transform to transaction devices. The evolution is happening faster than we think.

Mobile Usage Around the World is Not the Same

For every computer in the world, there are three mobile phones. Studies show that by 2010, there will be 4 billion mobile phones on this planet, and if we see the 2007 numbers, we may reach there well before 2010. 4 billion is 60% of the global population! Mobiles have provided an affordable and accessible computing platform. For most users, their mobile phone is their primary connection with high-tech, and more importantly the Web!

At the same time, the maturity of the mobile market differs widely in different regions. Japan and Korea are the most advanced, whereas Brazil, Russia, India, and China are seeing a volume growth. In developed countries, most people have exposure to computers and they adopt mobile web applications faster. In developing countries, communication and entertainment applications are proving more successful. There is a huge potential for low-cost services that can benefit large portions of the population.

When you build your mobile web application, make sure you understand the market well and launch the product accordingly. You may be too early or too late otherwise!

Mobiles and Desktops

When people access the Web from their mobile phones, they are in a different context. They may be traveling, waiting for something else to happen, looking for a nearby restaurant, wanting to take care of some chore or just browsing for fun. Mobiles are hardly used like the typical desktop is. Here is the first lesson to learn in mobile web application development:

People Use Their Mobiles Differently Than Their Desktops

Let's take an example. When you are at your desktop, you are doing one thing—using the computer for the job at hand. You have a large screen which can represent a multitude of information. You are used to seeing a lot of information on the page, scanning it quickly with your eyes, and then clicking on something that looks useful. You have access to broadband internet connection and can experience multimedia content fully. You may be running a few applications on your computer and may have a few tabs open in your browser.

Now, you want to find out something about the latest Harry Potter movie. You open a new tab in your browser, and do a Google search for it. You see a list of reviews about the movie, the storyline, and the cast. You may jump up to IMDB in another tab and review the details. You may open the movie site to view a preview. You think it's a watchable movie. So you call up your wife to check if Saturday evening would be good for her and the kids. She confirms. Then you think you should check with your neighborhood buddy too—he was talking about taking his kids to the movie too. So you pull up your instant messenger and send him a message. He says it will work! So you can now book the tickets. You do another Google search to find out movie theaters running Harry Potter around your home. You find two. You compare the timings and decide on one. After a few screens to make the movie selection, timings, and the number of tickets, you punch in your credit card number to make payment. It processes the request over a secure connection and shows you the confirmation screen. You click to see a printable ticket, print it, and keep it with you, not forgetting to inform your kids, your wife, and the friend that tickets are booked. The following figure shows this process.

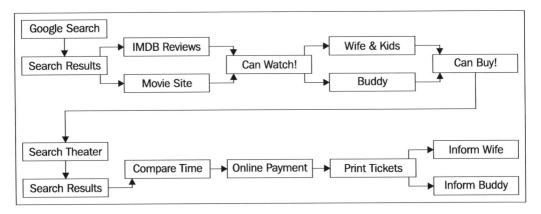

How Would You Do This Using Your Mobile?

First, when would you use your mobile to do something like this? When you use your mobile to do a Google search on the Harry Potter movie, most probably you are looking for a nearby movie theater to go and watch the movie today evening! Would you like to research on the movie, the cast, and what the latest issue of E! wrote about them while you are rushing to your office, holding your bag in one hand and a newspaper in another? Would you like to view the movie preview when loading a simple page takes 30 seconds? Would you like to instant message your friend and engage in four screen long e-commerce experience when you don't have a mouse or keyboard, and the only way to enter information is 12 numeric keys and 4 arrow keys? Most probably not!

Most of the actions you would do from a desktop to buy movie tickets will not be convenient from a mobile. It is too cumbersome to go through long pages using a set of arrow keys. We will need a recharge of patience if we wanted to watch a movie preview on low speed mobile networks. We may be more comfortable with something like this:

You are traveling back home, and recall you promised to take the kids for a movie tonight. It's been a busy day and you couldn't buy tickets during the week. You pull out your phone, and fire up the browser. You load up Google and do a search for Harry Potter. It shows you a simple page with the movie title at the top, star rating, and a three-line description of the plot. This is followed by a list of five movie theaters around this location and timings at which they are showing the movie tonight. You think your neighborhood buddy might be interested in the movie as well. So you back out from the browser a bit and call him up to find out. He confirms. You come back to the browser, and select the third theater by hitting 3 on your keypad. Next, you enter the number of people and select the show—again with the numeric keypad. You get a confirmation screen to book the tickets, you confirm by pressing a key on the phone. It sends out an SMS to the theater placing the order. Within moments, you get an MMS informing that the tickets are booked; you will see the charge in your next phone bill. Attached is an image with some bar code. You save the message and send an SMS to your kids, your wife and your friend that you are going for the movie tonight!

Once you reach the movie theater, you show the barcode image through your phone. The bar code reader recognizes it and prints you the tickets. You buy some popcorn and enjoy the movie with your friends and family.

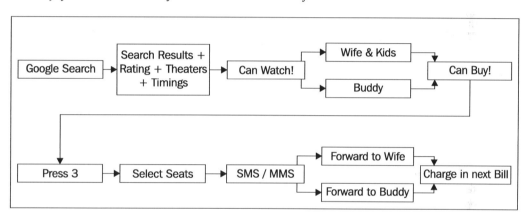

The tasks people want done using their desktop computers are different from the ones they want to get done using their mobile phones. The resources available at a desktop computer are much different from those of a mobile. You may use the desktop computer for longer research. You may use the mobile for quick messaging and on-the-go tasks. You may use mobile web to read up your email, search for a few things, look up the price of your favorite stock, send a quick message or two, stay in touch with your friends, blog about what you are up to or quickly book a movie ticket!

Subscribers also have to pay for mobile usage; most would not prefer to stay online for long times unless they have unlimited access plans. Mobile usability is one of the biggest hurdles in mobile web, and it requires careful planning of not just the content, but also the navigation, clicks, input required, and the time it will take to carry out a task. We will discuss mobile usability and related best practices in detail in the next chapters.

It's Not All Rosy—Mobile Devices have Limitations

It becomes critical to understand mobile usability not just because users are in a different context when they access mobile web, but also because mobile devices have their own limitations. Mobiles are not full-fledged computers. On top of it, each mobile device is different. Manufacturers have to distinguish their devices for them to sell. Network operators sometimes offer customized phones, and they are tied heavily into their way of things.

Typical mobile devices have screen sizes from 120x120 pixels up to 320x240. This means you can show about 6 lines of 25 characters in a screen! They may have a QWERTY keyboard or stylus, or have just the numeric keypad for input. They may not have processors that can deal with complicated calculations or even the RAM to hold your entire page before rendering it! They may support only a limited set of image and multimedia formats—e.g. Animated GIFs are not supported on most phones. Different browsers will render the same page differently—some will strip out formatting completely, while some will shrink the display to fit the smaller size of the device. Some will remove images and some may not work with access key-based links. Some have a 9.6kbps link to the Internet, some have higher. Some may support handheld CSS, while some may only support WML. A device comes from design to market in 18 months, so manufacturers skip upgrading current devices to push newer models.

This means that there are millions of devices with differing capabilities that may access your mobile website. And you have got to make sure that your site looks and works OK with them. You not only have to test with many browsers, emulators, and actual devices, but you have to keep listening to your users and make adjustments accordingly.

Advantages of Mobile Web

Despite all the limitations, there are certainly advantages to using mobile web. The biggest benefit is that the user can access information anytime, anywhere, and when she or he wants. It frees her or him from the boundaries of the desktop and allows accomplishing tasks from anywhere. Because it can be used from anywhere, a mobile phone knows its location. This means we can develop location-sensitive applications, for example, showing restaurants in three blocks of where the user is. And as most of the mobile devices have phone capabilities, mobile web can be used to start a call or message to take quick action.

And as we have already seen, the number of mobile phones is more than thrice that of computers in the world. Mobile web can be the means to bridge the digital divide, to bring the power of computer and internet to the rest of the world.

But There are Many Ways to Do Mobile Web Development!

You have a good set of options when you want to develop for mobile devices. You can develop platform-specific applications that subscribers may download. These applications may internally connect to the net and perform some operations. J2ME (Java 2 Platform Mobile Edition), Symbian, or BREW/uiOne from Qualcomm can be used for mobile web development. Adobe's Flash Lite is another platform that's gaining acceptance.

Yet, the most common method of developing for mobile web is using XHTML (Extensible Hypertext Markup Language) and WML (Wireless Markup Language). Use of content-only markups like RSS and other micro-formats is also on a rise. With this, the device itself can decide how to present the information, while the website only provides the content.

What About WAP?

If you have been around the technology industry for a while, you may remember the hype around mobile web and WAP in the 1999 – 2000 days—just before the bubble burst. You may also remember the phone Neo used in the movie The Matrix. That phone was Nokia 7100, the first phone to support WAP—Wireless Access Protocol. WAP is the protocol to access the Internet from a mobile device. It provided an XML based language—Wireless Markup Language (WML), using which you could do mobile web application development.

Though served over normal HTTP server, the WAP architecture has a gateway between the server and the client. This gateway encodes the content in binary form to save bandwidth before sending it to the client and allows monitoring usage by the service provider.

The WAP specifications have evolved over time, and the standard now is WAP 2.0. This adopts an XHTML variant—XHTML Mobile Profile (XHTML-MP). XHTML-MP offers richer presentation and is very similar to HTML. We are going to use XHTML-MP for this book.

Bringing Order with Standards and Guidelines

The only way to bring order to the chaos in mobile development is to establish standards and guidelines. W3C's Mobile Web Initiative has been instrumental in this. It has best practices for mobile web development, and also a specification mobileOK to determine whether your site can work on various mobiles or not.

XHTML Mobile Profile is the standard language for mobile web development. XHTML-MP is built on top of XHTML Basic. W3C developed XHTML Basic originally for mobile devices but Open Mobile Alliance (OMA) added support for WAP CSS (WCSS) and other usability enhancements over XHTML Basic and defined it as XHTML-MP. Hence XHTML-MP has been adopted as a standard by device manufacturers. Most phones support it.

There are many opinions about mobile web development today. Because the need is to show mobile web content in an acceptable manner to a wide variety of handsets and browsers, the two most common practices are "adaptation" and "lowest common denominator".

Adaptation, sometimes called multiserving, means delivering content as per the device's capabilities. Adapt the content to suit the device so that it looks best to the user. Different techniques are used for adaptation—including detection, redirection, setting correct MIME types, changing links, and removing or scaling graphics. The "lowest common denominator" or LCD method establishes a minimum set of features expected from the device and develops content adhering to those guidelines. The minimum expected feature set is also called the Default Delivery Context (DDC).

W3C-Defined Default Delivery Context

- Usable Screen Width: 120 pixels, minimum
- Markup Language Support: XHTML Basic 1.1 delivered with content type application/xhtml+xml
- Character Encoding: UTF-8
- Image Format Support: JPEG, GIF 89a
- Maximum Total Page Weight: 20 kilobytes
- Colors: 256 Colors minimum
- Style Sheet Support: CSS Level 1. In addition, CSS Level 2 *@media* rule together with the *handheld* and *all* media types
- HTTP: HTTP/1.0 or more recent HTTP 1.1
- Script: No support for client-side scripting

Adaptation is Better, but LCD is Easier

Adapting according to the device capabilities is the ideal solution for delivering mobile web. At the same time, most developers will want to first achieve LCD before doing adaptation. The reasons for going with the lowest common denominator are many. Adaptation involves extra cost and complexity. It also requires changes on the server side to detect and deliver content; this may not be possible for all. If you are doing mobile development for the first time, it may not be easy to adapt. LCD may also be sufficient in cases where usage of the mobile site is limited.

For our examples, we will start with LCD and move to adaptation in later chapters.

Summary

We have quite a few basics in place now, so let's do a quick review:

- Things are moving mobile! There are already successful mobile web applications.
- Mobiles will reach 60% of the world population by 2010. For many users, this will be the first exposure to high tech and internet. A mobile device will be their first computer!
- Mobile data usage around the world is growing exponentially.
- Mobile web is about delivering the Web to mobile, and to utilize features of the mobile platform.
- Mobile devices come in all shapes in sizes—features, screen sizes, input, connectivity, multimedia, etc.
- Mobile usability is a big challenge—people use mobiles differently from their desktops.
- XHTML-MP is the standard language for mobile web development.
- Adaptation is the ideal method for content delivery, but lowest common denominator may work.
- The opportunity for mobile web is huge!

So let's go ahead and start developing some mobile web content!

2
Starting Your Mobile Site

Now is the time for us to start developing mobile web applications. In this chapter, we will get our first look at the example site we'll be building in the book: "Pizza On The Run". Specifically, we will look at:

- Picking the best method to deliver your site to mobile browsers
- Designing navigation and information architecture
- Setting up a development environment
- Learning XHTML Mobile Profile—the presentation language for mobile applications
- Developing Pizza On The Run's mobile site homepage

By the end of the chapter, you will have a solid foundation for building complex, powerful mobile sites.

Pizza On The Run and the Mobile Web

Luigi Mobeeli owns Pizza On The Run—a small-time pizza shop in Sunnyvale. Luigi cooks some delicious pizzas, just like his parents who started the shop. Situated in the heart of Silicon Valley, POTR is hugely popular amongst geeks because of its quick delivery and round-the-clock service. With so many geek friends around, Luigi caught on to technology early. About 25% of POTR orders come through the website. But Luigi is not very happy.

Close to 70% of the customers picked up a phone and ordered their pizzas. Luigi knew many by name, and even their favorite pizzas. He could guess what they would order and where to deliver just by the hearing their name. But the business was growing and he couldn't always take the calls. Many customers had to wait a long time to get through the line, and then spend more time figuring out what to order. When Luigi ran some special offers, the time per order on the phone went up as well—understanding the offer and then deciding to opt for it.

POTR needed something better, faster, and more efficient. And Luigi had an idea! What if he automated the whole process? What problems would it solve if a customer could order a pizza on her way to the coffee machine?

Luigi knew that customers want to place an order as quickly as possible. When not in the "transaction mode", they may want to find out about special offers or go through details of various menu options. And that's pretty much all they may want from the mobile version of POTR website. It would also be great if they could just repeat one of their last orders!

So Luigi wants to let people order pizza using their mobile browsers. What could he do?

Different Options for Going Mobile

If you want to deliver your website to mobile devices, you essentially have four options.

1. Do nothing: just leave the site as it is and let the user's mobile browser render it.

2. Remove formatting: simplify the site so that it loads faster and uses less bandwidth, but leave the design the same.

3. CSS-based design: use a different Cascading Style Sheet file for mobile visitors and define mobile optimized formatting of various page elements through this CSS.

4. Create a new site: develop a version of your site tailored for mobile browsers and people on the move.

What is CSS?

A Cascading Style Sheet (CSS) is a way to define the visual appearance of different HTML elements. You can specify the size, color, and position of standard HTML elements like `<body>`, `<p>`, `<td>`, etc. as well as sections you define using a name or `id`. CSS has become the preferred way of formatting well structured HTML code over the years because it facilitates having standard design throughout the website, and managing it from a single file.

Let's look at each of these in turn…

Do Nothing

This may sound surprising, but many mobile browsers can render websites well on the small screen. Most notably the techniques adopted in Opera's Small Screen Rendering (SSR), Apple's iPhone, and the new Nokia Browser deliver very good results. Browsers may scale down the website display at the client side, or pass it through a server-side routine that will make necessary adjustments to the HTML and images. Some browsers simply remove all the CSS and formatting information while showing the main text and links to the user. If you do nothing, your website may still be visible on a mobile browser, though it may not look and function as you may want. Luigi had already noticed visitors using mobile browsers in the website statistics and even received orders through such customers.

When to Use This Approach

- You don't expect enough people coming to the site from a mobile device.
- Most of your users are using Smartphones or other large-screen devices with a capable browser.
- People want to use your website just the way they use it on their desktop; they don't want any mobile-specific features.
- You do not have the time or resources to use other methods!

When to Avoid This Approach

- You want to reach the maximum number of potential customers.
- When people access your site from a mobile device they have a specific task at hand that they need done fast.
- You want to deliver the best experience to your mobile customers!

Remove Formatting

One of the biggest difficulties for mobile browsers is to parse the HTML and lay out the page. Complex formatting rules mean more computing operations, and this may not be available to small devices because of limited CPU and RAM. Most mobile subscribers also pay bandwidth charges per kilobyte, so heavy HTML and images will make a big hole in their pockets. If we make a "vanilla flavor" of a website, removing formatting, images, objects, and other complications, it would display reasonably well on any mobile browser.

There are even tools that allow you to do this easily. IYHY.com, Skweezer.net, and Mike Davidson's PHP include files that can make your site mobile-friendly in just two minutes (`http://www.mikeindustries.com/blog/archive/2005/07/make-your-site-mobile-friendly`). Note that your site may not look pretty with this approach! More often than not, you end up with pages full of text links and URLs.

When to Use This Approach

- You want a quick and dirty way to make your site mobile-usable!

- You want to cover most mobile browsers.

- Your site is mainly text and has a good navigation structure.

When to Avoid This Approach

- When the site needs good UI design. You don't want the visitors scrolling pages full of text.

- When the majority of the content is not really useful for a mobile visitor.

CSS-Based Design

If you don't want to keep two versions of your site, yet deliver a usable site on a mobile, you can control the lay out of the site using CSS. First, develop your site in a standard web browser; make sure you lay out the content effectively using CSS. CSS allows positioning of content in any way that you want, even if the content is not written in that order in the XHTML. But this is a pitfall with CSS; ensure that your XHTML code is well structured and in the order you want to show the content. This will make it easier for browsers that load CSS once content is loaded and apply formating after that.

Once you have got this far, the next step is to add an alternative CSS to be used when the site is accessed from a handheld device. This solution is a recommended approach for many simple needs. It also adheres to the W3C principle of Device Independence—delivering the same content to any device. Luigi thinks this can be a good way to start his mobile site—in any case most of the current site is based on CSS, so he just needs to add an extra CSS file!

Here's how you can add an alternative stylesheet link in your XHTML page:

```
<link rel="stylesheet" type="text/css" media="handheld"
href="mobile.css">
```

Notice the use of `media` attribute. It tells the browser to use this CSS only if it is a handheld browser.

Wireless CSS

Wireless CSS (WCSS) is a special derivative of CSS for mobile devices. It supports most of the CSS 2 properties, and contains some additional properties for mobile devices. These include some animation effects and input formatting rules. We will learn more about WCSS in the next chapter.

When to Use This Approach

- You want the same content and information architecture delivered on both desktop and mobile, with formatting changes to suit the device.
- You want a simple and effective way to deliver on the mobile.
- You already have a lot of content styled using CSS and want to quickly make it available on mobile.

When to Avoid This Approach

- You do not want visitors to incur heavy bandwidth charges by downloading all the images.
- Your site visitors do not use a mobile browser that supports CSS.
- The current site uses tables for most of the formatting, rather than CSS.

Mobile Site

Finally, you can have a full fledged version for mobile browsers. Scaling down the display of the site or presenting the same content of a site to a mobile user is not always the best thing. The expectations of a mobile user are very different from those of a desktop user. As we discussed in the first chapter, when you Google for a movie from a mobile device, you most probably want to book a ticket, rather than reading long reviews and controversies. This means when you develop sites for mobile devices, you should tailor not only the design, but also the navigation, flow, and content. You can even go to the extent of adapting presentation depending on the capabilities of mobile device. This is the panacea of mobile web delivery.

When to Use This Approach

- When you want to deliver the most usable experience to the user.
- When you want to use phone-specific features like invoking a phone call.
- When many users will access the site from a mobile for a particular task. And you want to make sure they can get the job done fast.
- When you want to deliver smaller files to mobiles to facilitate faster browsing.
- When it makes business sense to spend the time and resources on the effort.

When to Avoid This Approach

- When most of the users are using the site from their desktop computers.

- There is no real need for accessing the site from a mobile.

- You want to avoid the efforts, learning curve, and the overhead involved.

Luigi is now clear that he wants to deliver the best experience to his customers. Rather than moving the full site to a mobile version, he decides to do only a portion of it—parts that a mobile web user would be interested in. This boils down to making it easy to order pizzas by developing a mobile-specific site, and providing a link to the normal site for people who want to know more.

Luigi has also figured out that XHTML Mobile Profile (XHTML MP) is the best method to build his mobile site. It converges web with mobile and the biggest advantage is that the same technologies, tools, and skills used to develop websites can be used to develop for mobile web delivery. So he and his geek friend can easily pull together a mobile version of the site using their existing capabilities. It will even be easy to port the existing site to the mobile version with minor changes.

Luigi has a lot of work ahead, so let's see what's next!

Mobile Navigation and Information Architecture

We now know that a mobile web user has different goals while accessing a site. He/She may not be looking for a lot of information, and wants to complete the task at hand. Different mobile devices have different capabilities and we must take care of that while designing our mobile website.

This poses different challenges for the information architecture and navigation of a mobile site.

Step-By-Step: Planning the Structure of Your Mobile Site

- **Define user personas**: Who is going to use the site? What's the target market? In what circumstances will they come to the site? What's the context? List down typical users who would use the application.

- **Define user goals**: What tasks do they want to achieve on the site? Is there a better way of achieving these goals than a typical website flow? Why would they want to do this task over a mobile? How does your mobile site help them accomplish their goals?

- **Define target devices**: Do you want to limit to a particular set of devices? Or use some device-specific feature? Do you want to use SMS/Phone capabilities?

- **Do paper prototypes**: Sketch out the workflow for accomplishing user goals on paper (yes, pen and paper are still useful!).

- **Test with real users**: Show the prototype to real users and get their feedback. Make modifications, accordingly.

- **Make XHTML prototype and test again**: After you've passed the paper prototyping round, convert the prototypes into XHTML MP. Now test them on target mobile devices. Test them also with real users and make modifications till you get things right.

Let's think about the Pizza On The Run application to understand this better. POTR is similar to a shopping cart. In typical online e-commerce systems, you will have a shopping cart, you will browse products, and add items you like to the cart. You then move to checkout, make the payment, and complete the transaction. If we take the same approach on POTR, we will have a browse option to review the menu details, an add-to-cart button on each product page, a shopping cart to review the order, and the checkout process.

What could be a better way to order pizzas? Luigi says the users want to order pizzas quickly. They do not want confusion. It is best to present limited content and allow them to make quick choices that lead to the final order. In the case of side dishes and beverages, we can actually show the full list of choices available, most popular at the top, and users can check off the ones they want. It would also be a good idea to offer to repeat the last order.

While structuring a mobile site, we must spend enough time on information architecture design. If the user has to spend too much time to locate the information he/she wants, they may get bugged and go away. No businessman would like that! Mr. Mobeeli is certainly not going to allow that! Then, how about a structure like this?

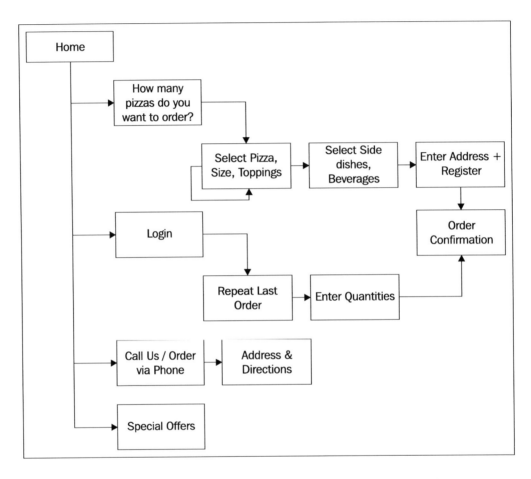

We have prioritized the order of available options on the homepage. The pizza ordering process is like a wizard, asking the user to take only a couple of decisions at each step. Mr. Mobeeli is going to be happy with this!

Handy Tips in Structuring Your Mobile Site

Here are a few tips you can keep in mind when you work on your mobile sites:

- Take a minimalistic approach. Remove everything that you can.

- Respect the user's time, money, and attention. Don't frustrate them.

- Do task-centered design! Focus on user goals.

- Give less choice—no long menus, no long options, no long pages.

- Maximum 10 links on a page.

- Navigation should be drill down, and contextual. Customize navigation according to the page. No more than 5 levels of drilling down!

- No pages with just links to drill down further. Make sure each page has valuable content. Even the homepage should have actionable content.

- Prioritize links and content. What's more important goes to the top.

- Always provide a way to exit to home, and step back in the footer.

- Break lengthy/complicated forms into a wizard like step-by-step process.

Setting Up the Development Environment

You can develop XHTML MP websites with any text editor. If you use an HTML editor with code completion, syntax highlighting, and validation—it will be perfect for mobile web development. You may want to have a good CSS editor and an image manipulation program like Photoshop or Gimp too. Overall, your current web development tools will work!

If you are going to use server-side processing for your application, you will need a server-side setup. This could be PHP, .NET, JSP, Ruby, Python, Perl or any other language. The server-side code should output XHTML MP code instead of HTML. During testing, a setup on your machine accessible from `http://localhost` will work well.

You can use a desktop web browser to test the application—since it is XHTML. It's a good practice to test your application first in a browser, then in a mobile device simulator. A simulator will allow you to run your application as if it is running from a mobile device. You can test for different screen sizes and also use the keypad to get a feel of how the user will be using the application. There are a number of simulators/emulators available. Desktop simulators will allow you to test from localhost, but web-based ones require you to upload your files on a server and test from there. Most desktop simulators are Windows only, so you may need access to a Windows system to run them.

Here are the links for the sites from where you can download them:

- Openwave Phone Simulator — `http://developer.openwave.com/`.

- Yospace SmartPhone Emulator — great collection of devices to simulate. A browser-based demo: `http://www.yospace.com/spedemo.html`.

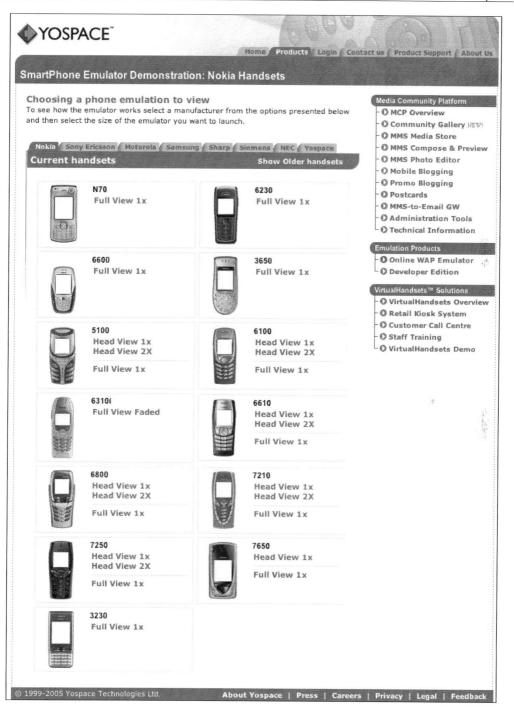

- Opera Mini Simulator—a wonderful Java applet-based simulator that you can run within your browser. Works the same way as the actual Opera Mini browser, http://www.opera.com/products/mobile/operamini/demo.dml.

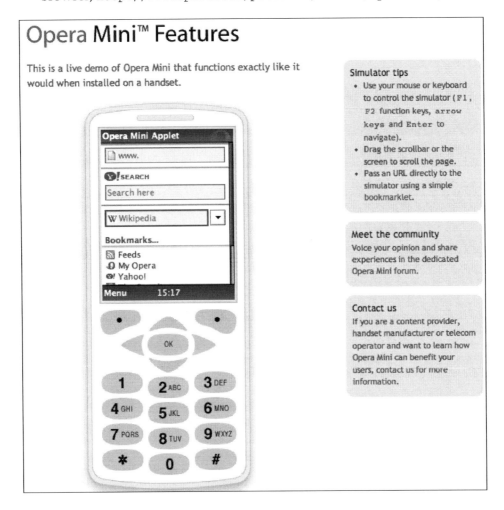

- Nokia Mobile Internet Toolkit includes a simulator—look for **Tools and SDKs** on http://www.forum.nokia.com/ and **Browsing Tools** in that.
- You can also find Motorola's tools from http://www.motocoder.com/ and Sony Ericsson's from http://www.ericsson.com/mobilityworld.

Note that nothing beats a real mobile! So once you have tested your site with simulators, test it with some real mobile devices. You will be able to understand your users' real experience only in this way. As a matter of fact, test early and often, on real devices.

There is another interesting thing you will notice when you test on different devices! Different devices have different browsers, and different browser versions have different features (and bugs). You will experience a wide variety in terms of colors, fonts, layout and table support, image handling, and standards compliance—in other words, you may have many hair pulling experiences making things work on different devices! But you will learn a lot! You need to host the application on the public Internet to test from real devices, and it will also give you the opportunity to test the speed of the application.

DeviceAnywhere is a cheap and effective way to test on real devices!

One great service that allows you to test on a variety of real devices is DeviceAnywhere (`www.deviceanywhere.com`). They give you access to real devices from your desktop computer. You also have more than 300 devices that you can choose from, and quite a few network operators. Using the DeviceAnywhere Studio, you can connect to a remote device. The Studio will take input from your desktop to the device and stream the output screens from the device back to your desktop. This is a superb way of testing on real devices at a fraction of the cost!

Bottomline: It's best to test with actual devices, but test on five different simulators as well.

Hosting Your Mobile Site is Trivial

If you are wondering how to put up your site on a server to access it from browser-based simulators and real devices, don't worry! You can host your mobile site just like a normal site. Unlike the old days, you do not have to do any special server setup. You can simply FTP the files to your server, and access them from a mobile browser.

There is also a special top-level domain for mobile sites—.mobi. You can buy that, and also host your site with dotMobi (`www.dotmobi.com`). One recommendation is to keep the mobile site URL short, so that users can easily type it.

`http://m.sitename.com` is better than `http://www.sitename.com/mobile/` You can also implement a browser detection routine on `http://www.sitename.com/` that automatically redirects the user to the mobile version of the site if they access it from a mobile device.

POTR Mobile Homepage

Luigi is now excited to build his mobile site. Let's put up a "coming soon" page for him. Check the following code.

```
<?xml version="1.0" encoding="UTF-8"?>
<!DOCTYPE html PUBLIC "-//WAPFORUM//DTD XHTML Mobile 1.0//EN"
"http://www.wapforum.org/DTD/xhtml-mobile10.dtd">
<html xmlns="http://www.w3.org/1999/xhtml">
  <head>
    <title>Luigi's Pizza On The Run</title>
  </head>
  <body>
    <img src="potr_logo.jpg" width="120" height="42"
    alt="Luigi's Pizza On The Run" />
    <p>Mobile ordering coming soon!</p>
    <p>If you're already hungry, call
    <a href="wtai://wp/mc;+18007687669">+1-800-POTRNOW</a></p>
  </body>
</html>
```

Here's how the code will show up in Openwave browser simulator:

and in Opera's desktop web browser in Small screen mode:

Making a Call is as Simple as Email

Did you notice the link on the POTR homepage to make a call? If the user wants to place an order, she or he can simply follow the link and get connected to Luigi's shop. Most mobile devices can make a call or send a text message. Adding a call link is as simple as a `mailto` link! Here's the code to do a single-click call:

```
<a href="wtai://wp/mc;+18007687669">+1-800-POTRNOW</a>
```

There is a simpler method as well:

```
<a href="tel:+18007687669">+1-800-POTRNOW</a>
```

Either of these will work on most devices. Some phones do not support it, and some others work with one method. You may need to use device-based adaptation to determine the best way (and we will learn to do that in the fourth chapter). If you want to keep things simple, just go ahead with the `tel` method.

Understanding the Homepage

You may have noticed the similarities between HTML and XHTML MP code by now! The homepage also shows up as the same in both mobile and desktop browsers. Let us examine different parts of the code now.

Document Structure

The first two lines of the code are the XHTML prolog. They declare the XML version and the DOCTYPE of the document. The DOCTYPE specifies the DTD (Document Type Definition) for the XML document—defining the grammatical rules for the XML that follows. A validating browser may download the DTD and check that against the XML to ensure it's in proper format. The character set in the XML declaration line tells the language encoding for the file. You should be fine with UTF-8 in most cases. Also, notice that you do not need to close these two elements;

```
<?xml version="1.0" encoding="UTF-8"?>
<!DOCTYPE html PUBLIC "-//WAPFORUM//DTD XHTML Mobile 1.0//EN"
"http://www.wapforum.org/DTD/xhtml-mobile10.dtd">
```

The rest is very much like HTML. It is mandatory for an XHTML MP document to have `html`, `head`, `title`, and `body` elements. You can specify `meta` tags and other document-specific information within the head element. The body element must have at least one element in it.

Yes, it's that simple!

Fundamentals of XHTML MP

Now that we have seen how the homepage works, let us learn some more about XHTML MP.

Before Writing Further Code, Let's Learn Some Grammar

Since XHTML MP is based on XHTML, certain syntactical rules must be followed. Making syntactical errors is a good way to learn a programming language, but so that you don't get frustrated with them, here are some rules you must follow with XHTML MP! Remember, HTML is very forgiving in terms of syntax, but make a small syntax error in XHTML MP and the browser may refuse to show your page!

Overall, XHTML elements consist of a start tag—element name and its attributes, element content, and closing tag. The format is like:

```
<element attribute="value">element content</element>
```

XHTML Documents Must be Well Formed

Since XHTML is based on XML, all XHTML documents must adhere to the asic XML syntax and be well formed. The document must also have a DOCTYPE declaration.

Tags Must be Closed!

All open tags must be closed. Even if it is an empty tag like "<br>", it must be used in the self-closed form like "<br />". Note the extra space before the slash. It's not mandatory, but makes things work with some older browsers. If you can validate within your editor, make it a practice to do that. Also cultivate the habit of closing a tag that you start immediately—even before you put in the content. That will ensure you don't miss closing it later on!

Elements Must be Properly Nested

You cannot start a new paragraph until you complete the previous one. You must close tags to ensure correct nesting. Overlapping is not allowed. So the following is not valid in XHTML MP:

```
<p><b>Pizzas are <i>good</b>.</i></p>
```

It should be written as:

```
<p><b>Pizzas are <i>good</i>.</b></p>
```

Elements and Attributes Must be in Lowercase

XHTML MP is case sensitive. And you must keep all the element tags and all their attributes in lowercase, although values and content can be in any case.

Attribute Values Must be Enclosed within Quotes

HTML allowed skipping the quotation marks around attribute values. This will not work with XHTML MP as all attribute values must be enclosed within quotes—either single or double. So this will not work:

```
<div align=center>Let things be centered!</div>
```

It must be written as:

```
<div align="center">Let things be centered!</div>
```

Attributes Cannot be Minimized

Consider how you would do a drop down in HTML:

```
<select>
<option value="none">No toppings</option>
<option value="cheese" selected>Extra Cheese</option>
<option value="olive">Olive</option>
<option value="capsicum">Capsicum</option>
</select>
```

The same drop down in XHTML is done as:

```
<select>
<option value="none">No toppings</option>
<option value="cheese" selected="selected">Extra Cheese</option>
<option value="olive">Olive</option>
<option value="capsicum">Capsicum</option>
</select>
```

The "selected" attribute of the "option" element has only one possible value and, with HTML, you can minimize the attribute and specify only the attribute without its value. This is not allowed in XHTML, so you must specify the attribute as well as its value, enclosed in quotes. Another similar case is the "checked" attribute in check boxes.

XHTML Entities Must be Handled Properly

If you want to use an ampersand in your XHTML code, you must use it as `&amp;` and not just `&`.

& is used as a starting character for HTML entities — e.g. ` `, `&quot;`, `&lt;`, `&gt;` etc. Just using & to denote an ampersand confuses the XML parser and breaks it. Similarly, use proper HTML Entities instead of quotation marks, less than/greater than signs, and other such characters. You can refer to `http://www.webstandards.org/learn/reference/charts/entities/` for more information on XHTML entities.

Most Common HTML Elements are Supported

The following table lists different modules in HTML and the elements within them that are supported in XHTML MP version 1.2. You can use this as a quick reference to check what's supported.

Module	Element
Structure	`body, head, html, title`
Text	`abbr, acronym, address, blockquote, br, cite, code, dfn, div, em, h1, h2, h3, h4, h5, h6, kbd, p, pre, q, samp, span, strong, var`
Presentation	`b, big, hr, i, small`
Style Sheet	`style` element and `style` attribute
Hypertext	`a`
List	`dl, dt, dd, ol, ul, li`
Basic Forms	`form, input, label, select, option, textarea, fieldset, optgroup`
Basic Tables	`caption, table, td, th, tr`
Image	`img`
Object	`object, param`
Meta Information	`meta`
Link	`link`
Base	`base`
Legacy	`start` attribute on `ol`, `value` attribute on `li`

Most of these elements and their attributes work as in HTML. Table support in mobile browsers is flaky, so you should avoid tables or use them minimally. We will discuss specific issues of individual elements as we go further.

XHTML MP Does Not Support Many WML Features

If you have developed WAP applications, you would be interested in finding the differences between WML (Wireless Markup Language—the predecessor of XHTML MP) and XHTML MP; apart from the obvious syntactical differences. You need to understand this also while porting an existing WML-based application to XHTML MP. Most of WML is easily portable to XHTML MP, but some features require workarounds. Some features are not supported at all, so if you need them, you should use WML instead of XHTML MP. WML 1.x will be supported in any mobile device that conforms to XHTML MP standards.

Here is a list of important WML features that are not available in XHTML MP:

- There is no metaphor of decks and cards. Everything is a page. This means you cannot pre-fetch content in different cards and show a card based on some action. With XHTML MP, you either have to make a new server request for getting new content, or use named anchors and link within the page.

- You could use the `<do>` tag in WML to program the left and right softkeys on the mobile device. Programming softkeys is not supported in XHTML MP; the alternative is to use `accesskey` attribute in the anchor tag (`<a>`) to specify a key shortcut for a link.

- WML also supports client-side scripting using WMLScript—a language similar to JavaScript. This is not supported in XHTML MP yet, but will come in near future in the form of ECMA Script Mobile Profile (ECMP).

- WML also supported client-side variables. This made it easier to process form data, validate them on the client side, and to reuse user-filled data across cards. This is not supported in XHTML MP.

- With XHTML MP, you have to submit a form with a submit button. WML allowed this on a link. WML also had a `format` attribute on the `input` tag—specifying the format in which input should be accepted. You need to use CSS to achieve this with XHTML MP.

- There are no timers in XHTML MP. This was a useful WML feature making it easier to activate certain things based on a timer. You can achieve a similar effect in XHTML MP using a meta refresh tag.

- The WML events ontimer, onenterbackward, onenterforward, and onpick are not available in XHTML MP. You can do a workaround for the ontimer event, but if you need others, you have to stick to using WML for development.

- XHTML MP also does not support the `<u>` tag, or `align` attribute on the `<p>` tag, and some other formatting options. All these effects can be achieved using CSS though.

Summary

In this chapter, we learned the basics of developing mobile web applications. We even created a temporary homepage for Luigi! Specifically, we learned:

- Different methods of mobile web development—doing nothing, simplification, CSS, and mobile-specific sites
- Designing information architecture and navigation for mobile
- Setting up a development environment, including simulators
- Hosting your mobile site
- Creating XHTML MP documents, the subset of XHTML that works on the web
- An easy way to make "clickable" phone numbers in your web apps
- Supported elements and language rules of XHTML MP

In the next chapter, we will implement most of the POTR mobile site. We will look at the graphic design and beautify our site using Wireless CSS!

Building Pizza On The Run

3

We are now ready to build a mobile pizza ordering system for Luigi's Pizza On The Run. We have the site structure chalked out, and have also done the basics of XHTML MP.

In this chapter, we will look at:

- Designing layouts for the mobile web
- Using Wireless CSS in design
- Being aware of differences in mobile browsers
- Creating the database and code architecture for POTR
- Using forms on the mobile web
- Handling user authentication
- Testing our work in simulators
- Constraining user input with Wireless CSS
- Applying special effects using Wireless CSS

By the end of the chapter, you will be able to build database-driven mobile web applications on your own.

Luigi's Pizza On The Run

Luigi has put up a teaser mobile homepage now, and posted a note about it on his website. Customers have already started calling via the mobile homepage. It's much easier for them to click a link and call! Luigi showed the proposed site structure to a few customers and they are excited to learn how quickly they can order through their mobiles. Luigi is now ready to build a full-fledged mobile pizza ordering system!

Designing Layouts for the Mobile Web

Design is an important element of any software. In today's competitive world, where everyone can offer the same service, design has become a differentiator. People want to look at beautifully designed pages; their confidence in the product is higher if it is well designed. How many of us would buy an iPhone just for its features? There are other phones that provide similar or better features, but we would like to have an iPhone because of its excellent design.

Web applications have witnessed many design trends. Designs in the sites that are often classified as Web 2.0 sites have gradients, rounded corners, large types, CSS designs, and fresh colors. This style of design has worked and designers now make desktop applications as well using such styles.

You certainly want to make your mobile website look beautiful. One of the first questions you have to answer is: what will be the size of the application? 1024x768 pixels is standard resolution of most desktops. What's the standard resolution for mobile devices? Well, it depends; let's look at why!

Mobile Screen Sizes

The pixel resolution available on mobiles is increasing. 176x208 pixels was the norm a while ago, but 240x320 is almost everywhere nowadays. Apple's iPhone is 320x480 and some Smartphones now sport a VGA resolution of 480x640 pixels (refer to the following figure). Within two years, mobiles may touch our current desktop resolutions.

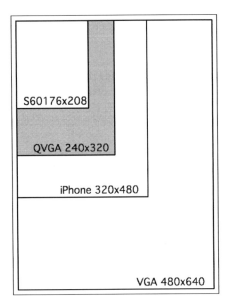

While the resolution is growing, the absolute screen size is not. Even if you have more pixels to play with, you only have 3 to 5 inches. Mobiles are also typically used at a hand's distance; something too small may not be usable. Mobile devices are normally taller than they are wide, and horizontal scrolling is not supported on some devices—so if the width of application is more than the device size, part of the application will not be shown. 150 pixels is a safe width for today, but you should check the target customers and the kind of device they will be using before making a decision.

Colors, Images, Page Sizes, and More

Expect at least 256 colors on a mobile device. Most mobiles support images well—GIF and JPG are universal. As the RAM and processor capabilities are limited, many devices keep a limit on the total size of a page—including WCSS, XHTML MP, and images. 10 kilobytes is the minimum you can expect, but it's best to keep the page sizes as small as possible—less than 30K is recommended. Many users browse with images turned off to save bandwidth costs. Hence our application must not rely on images for navigation or critical operations. Giving proper alternative text to images becomes a must.

We also need to remember the input and navigation methods while designing a mobile site—will the user have arrow keys for navigation or a stylus? Or would she or he be tapping with her or his fingers? It is critical to know your customers and design the site accordingly. Remember, mobile pages are not purely about design; they are more about functionality and usability! Remove all unnecessary images, CSS, and even XHTML code! Keep the design lean.

To Mobile or Not to Mobile?

Luigi is not sure what to do! He has seen Opera's small screen rendering that can scale and fold websites to show them neatly on a mobile browser. He's got himself an iPhone and likes the way Safari scales down websites. He keeps talking about how he can zoom in and pan by tapping and dragging fingers. Some of his friends are telling him about "One Web", and how users should have access to the same web content from any device—including mobile devices. He is confused. Should Luigi build a mobile version of the site or not?

Mobiles are becoming powerful and bandwidth cheaper. But then, how many people really have access to such powerful devices today? The majority are still using feature phones they bought a couple of years ago. They still have old browsers. But they do want to order pizzas from anywhere!

That's a very good argument, Luigi says. And he decides to go ahead with a mobile-specific version of Pizza On The Run. The design will be done keeping in mind a mobile user who wants to quickly order a pizza. We will keep things simple and easy, just focussing on getting the task done.

Web Layouts Don't Work on Mobile Devices

Typical webpage layouts won't fit mobile devices. Given there is no mouse or keyboard, and a small screen on the mobile device, we must choose a layout that can flow well. A website header normally has navigation links and branding graphics. But header links can be an overkill for mobiles. On most mobile browsers, you navigate by clicking the arrow key. You need to keep clicking to move from one link to another. Would you like to skip through 10 links to reach the actual content of the page? May be not! An ideal mobile web layout would flow vertically with distinct blocks for different page elements.

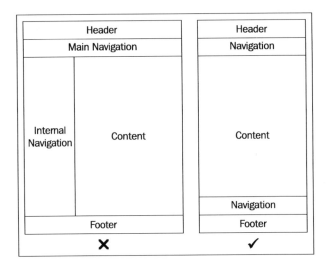

Simple links at the top of the page are great for the first page of a mobile site, and may not be needed on the inside pages. The sequence of clicks the user has to go through to reach a particular page (referred to as the clickstream) must be short. The most frequently used options should come up first. It's best to provide a header and minimal textual navigation at the top. Links to home and other important pages can be placed in the footer. Even the content should be broken down into easy-to-comprehend sections. You should avoid putting the same text content from your website onto the mobile web. It is best to rewrite the text copy of the site to serve the mobile users better.

Remember: As a mobile web developer, you must understand users. The entire design for the mobile site must be done for the user. Give them what they want and make it simple to get it. And keep learning from your experiences.

We will use simple vertical blocks for designing POTR. We will also keep images to the minimum and use clean XHTML code.

Using Wireless CSS as the Silver Bullet, Almost!

Most of us extensively use tables for layout design on websites. Tables are supported on most mobile browsers, but nested tables may not work. On the Web, CSS is preferred for designing page layouts. Fortunately, XHTML MP-compliant browsers too support Wireless CSS (WCSS), a subset of CSS 2.1. WCSS is very effective in controlling the layout of the site and should be used to flow the page in blocks and decorate elements. If you currently use CSS to style your documents, WCSS will not be a problem at all—it's just the same actually! We will talk about some special styles useful in mobile development as we build the POTR application. If you want to learn more about WCSS, Developers' Home has an excellent tutorial at: `http://www.developershome.com/wap/wcss/`.

You can style your current website to render well on a mobile device using CSS. You may hide certain portions with `display: none` or size images and text to fit well on a mobile device. However, keep in mind that even when you scale images or hide content blocks with CSS, they still download to the mobile browser before CSS is applied. This means your users may have to wait longer for the page to render and pay higher bandwidth charges.

Another important thing about CSS on mobile platforms: many browsers will render the page in two passes: first to load the content, and then to apply the style sheet. So the user may see basic HTML formatting before the style sheet is loaded and applied. This is especially true if you are loading an external style sheet.

Here are the five ways you can apply CSS in an XHTML MP page:

1. Linking to an external style sheet:

   ```
   <link rel="stylesheet" href="site.css"
   type="text/css" media="handheld">
   ```

2. Style definition within the document:

   ```
   <style type="text/css" media="handheld">...</style>
   ```

3. Document style sheet with @media qualifier:

```
<style type="text/css">
@media handheld { ... }
</style>
```

4. Importing an external style sheet to the document:

```
<style type="text/css">
@import url(...) handheld;
</style>
```

5. Inline style for an element:

```
<p style="align: left">Some text</p>
```

The preferred method is to link to an external style sheet and use inline styles to override. The following code defines the CSS we will use for POTR:

```
/* POTR Mobile Style sheet */
body, td, p {
    /* Most devices have their own fonts, but let's give it a shot */
    font-family: Verdana, Arial, Helvetica, sans-serif;
    font-size:1em
}
h1, h2 {
    color:#660033;
    border-bottom: 1px #000000 solid
}
h1 {
    font-size:1.4em
}
h2 {
    font-size:1.2em
}
h3 {
    font-size:1em;
    font-weight: bold
}
ul li {
    list-style: square
}
img {
    border: none
}
.error {
    color:#CC0000;
```

```css
    border: 1px #FF0000 solid;
    font-size: 0.8em;
    padding-left: 20px;
    background: left no-repeat url(error.gif)   #FFFF99
}
.debug {
    background-color:#EEEEEE;
    border: 1px #FF0000 solid
}
.button {
    border: 1px #FF6600 solid;
    background-color:#CCCCCC;
    font-size: 1.2em;
    font-weight: bold;
    margin-top: 0.5em;
    padding-left: 1em;
    padding-right: 1em
}
```

Consider that a mobile device may not have many fonts, especially not the ones we are used to. Typical devices have a few non-generic fonts, and at least one font from serif, sans-serif, and monospace families. Hence, our designs must not rely on particular fonts. When you are creating images and need to put text in them, bitmapped fonts will work better at small sizes.

Notice that we have used em as the measurement unit in most cases. Defining sizes relative to element size is very flexible and will render well across multiple browsers. We use standard heading tags and other HTML elements for formatting so that even if the browser does not have CSS support, our page will render acceptably.

We have defined custom styles for form buttons, errors, and debug messages. We have increased the size of the font in the button and given it some extra padding on the left and right to make the button larger. This will make it easier to locate and use the button.

How will this CSS look? Let's create a sample page and test it in different browsers.

```xml
<?xml version="1.0" encoding="UTF-8"?>
<!DOCTYPE html PUBLIC "-//WAPFORUM//DTD XHTML Mobile 1.0//EN"
                  "http://www.wapforum.org/DTD/xhtml-mobile10.dtd">
<html xmlns="http://www.w3.org/1999/xhtml">
<head>
<title>CSS / Forms Testpage</title>
<link rel="stylesheet" href="assets/mobile.css" type="text/css" />
</head>
<body>
<p class="error">Sorry, this is an error sample!</p>
<h1>h1 heading</h1>
<h2>h2 heading</h2>
```

```
<p>Normally you will have some text after the heading.
  This is a sample of that.</p>
<img src="assets/potr_logo.jpg" alt="Luigi's Pizza on the Run"
  width="120" height="42"/>
<h3>h3 heading</h3><p>Sample text after smaller heading.</p>
<table><tr><td>
<ul><li>List item</li><li>List item</li><li>List item</li></ul>
</td><td>
<ol><li>List item</li><li>List item</li><li>List item</li></ol>
</td></tr></table>
<form><fieldset>
Text field: <input type="text" /><br />
Select box: <select><option value="1">First option</option>
<option value="2">Second option</option><option value="3">Third
                                option</option></select><br />
<input type="radio" name="handsetType" checked="checked" />Phone
<input type="radio" name="handsetType" />SmartPhone<br />
Text area: <textarea rows="3" cols="30" name="details">Some
                                details here.</textarea><br />
<input type="checkbox" name="terms" value="1" />I agree
                                        to the terms<br />
<input type="submit" value="Send" class="button"/>
</fieldset></form>
</body></html>
```

Internet Explorer	Openwave	Opera Mini 4

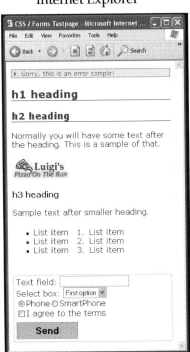

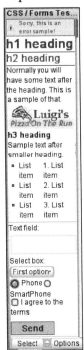

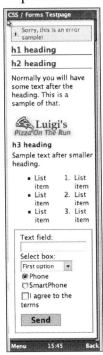

The CSS renders well for these browsers, though margins, font sizes, and form element rendering are inconsistent. Table support is present, and basic HTML elements render very well. The error message at the top has the most complicated CSS, but it shows up perfectly! Overall, we are good! We can now plan the back end for POTR.

Creating the Database and Code Architecture for POTR

We have learned the basics of graphic design and layout for mobile web applications. Now, we will build the back end for Pizza On The Run. We want to allow easy ordering of pizzas from mobile devices. We don't need to make the back end much different from what it would have been for a website, so we will quickly go through the common parts and look at the differences in detail.

Classes for POTR

We need to retrieve menu data from the database and save order information. We also need to provide user authentication. Most operations in our POTR site are related to the database, and are repeated. The Create, Retrieve, Update, and Delete (CRUD) operations are most common. So let us create a common class that others can extend—the common class will have all database-related functions and other frequently used methods.

One order can contain multiple pizzas. Each pizza has a base price and the user can customize the size, crust, and toppings, which add to the price. Thinking about all this, we can have a class structure as shown in the following figure:

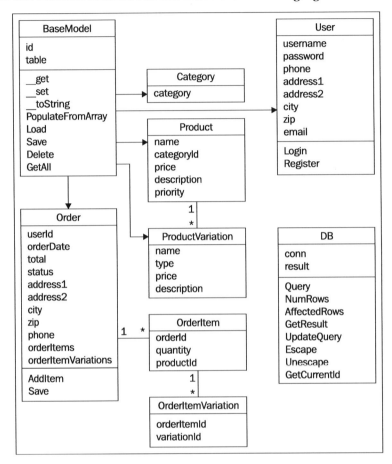

Database Schema

Deriving from the class structure, we can have a database schema as in the following figure. A few important notes:

- Product categories will be Pizzas, Side Dishes, and Beverages.

- The Products table will contain details of individual products. Variations are possible only on pizzas, so we don't need to relate them with all products.

- The variation type will decide what type of variation it is—Size, Crust, or Toppings.

- Each order may have one or more products in it, and if the order item is a pizza, it will have variations.

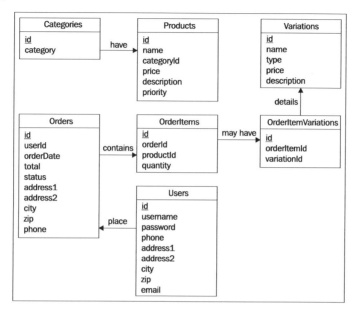

Coding Framework

We will use a simple fusebox-style coding framework. You may already be familiar with this style, but if you are not, it's easy to understand. Take a look at the following figure. All requests will pass through a central controller — index.php. Based on the value of the "action" variable, it will include another file. This action-specific file will carry out the business logic. At the end, the resulting XHTML will be sent back to the user's browser. Layout design is defined mainly in the header and footer files.

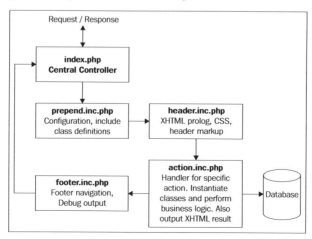

Redoing the POTR Homepage

We now know enough to start the actual code. The current POTR homepage promises people that online ordering will start soon. Let's start by spicing up the homepage! Our homepage file will be called `home.inc.php` and will be the default action.

Let's look at the various parts of `home.inc.php`.

```
<img src="assets/potr_logo.jpg" alt="Welcome to Luigi's Pizza On The
Run" width="120" height="42"/>
<ol>
<li><a href="#orderForm" accesskey="1">Order Pizzas</a></li>
<li><a href="#loginForm" accesskey="2">Login</a></li>
<li><a href="?action=contact" accesskey="4">Call Us / Directions</a></
li>
<li><a href="?action=offers" accesskey="4">Special Offers</a></li>
</ol>
```

The first line shows our logo. We then use an ordered list to show a navigation menu. This will make sure the menu shows consistently across browsers. The `accesskey` attribute in each link provides a shortcut key for that link. Pressing the 'accesskey' will activate a particular link without needing to navigate with arrows. We have ordered the links by priority so that the user can perform the desired action faster. The first two links point to forms on the same page, while the next two load a new page by passing the `action` parameter to the same `index.php` file. Notice that this navigation is only in the homepage. We do not repeat this on other pages; otherwise we could put this in the `header.inc.php`.

 The `"name"` attribute on `<a>` is not a valid XHTML MP markup. Use `"id"` instead for anchored links.

We start the ordering process right on the homepage. The following code shows the code for selecting the number of pizzas you want to order. On a mobile device, navigating through links is easier than using a select drop-down menu. So, we show normal links to select up to 4 pizzas. Then we provide a select box to select up to 9 pizzas. We use `selected="selected"` — full XHTML compliant form — to select 5 as default quantity in the drop down. All attributes are lower case and values are enclosed in double quotes. Also notice that & is escaped correctly in the links.

```
<a id="orderForm" />
<h2>Order:</h2>
<form method="post" action="index.php">
<fieldset>
<input type="hidden" name="action" value="order" />
```

```
<input type="hidden" name="step" value="1" />
<p>How many pizzas?
<a href="?action=order&amp;step=1&amp;numPizza=1">1</a> -
<a href="?action=order&amp;step=1&amp;numPizza=2">2</a> -
<a href="?action=order&amp;step=1&amp;numPizza=3">3</a> -
<a href="?action=order&amp;step=1&amp;numPizza=4">4</a> -
<select name="numPizza">
<option value="1">1</option>
<option value="2">2</option>
<option value="3">3</option>
<option value="4">4</option>
<option value="5" selected="selected">5</option>
<option value="6">6</option>
<option value="7">7</option>
<option value="8">8</option>
<option value="9">9</option>
</select>
<input type="submit" name="option" value="Select"/>
</fieldset>
</form>
</p>
```

On the homepage, we also want to show the login form. We include the `login.inc.php` file for this. We are including a separate file because the login form will be needed in the checkout process too. So if we have a separate file, we can use the same code at both these places.

```
<?php
include("login.inc.php");
?>
```

Let's s now see the code in `login.inc.php`.

```
<?php
// If we can find the username / password in the cookie (
//                           stored on last login), or if the page
// is called again - on a failed login - fill them up automatically
// Ideally, we should clean up and validate these variables
//                                    before using them
$myUsername = ($_COOKIE["potrUsername"] != "")? $_
COOKIE["potrUsername"] : $_POST["username"];
$myPassword = ($_COOKIE["potrPassword"] != "")? $_
COOKIE["potrPassword"] : $_POST["password"];
$returnUrl = isset($_REQUEST["return"]) ? $_REQUEST[
                                    "return"] : $return;
?>
```

```
<h2>Login</h2>
<p>Login to repeat your last orders and speed up checkout.</p>
<a id="loginForm" />
<form action="index.php" method="post">
<fieldset>
<input type="hidden" name="action" value="login" />
<input type="hidden" name="return" value="<?php
                                   echo $returnUrl; ?>" />
User: <input type="text" name="username" maxlength="15" value=
                        "<?php echo $myUsername; ?>" /><br />
Password: <input type="password" name="password" maxlength="15"
                value="<?php echo $myPassword; ?>" /><br />
<input type="checkbox" value="1" name="remember"
                checked="checked" />Remember login details<br />
<input type="submit" value="Login" />
</fieldset>
</form>
```

We allow saving the username and password in a cookie to automatically populate fields from the cookie, next time. We are not using cookies for authentication; just to store this information to make it faster to log in next time. Also, we do not want to make it mandatory to log in to select products. This may be a roadblock in usability. In the ordering process, we will give an option to register automatically if the user wants. After the first order, she or he can log in either at the start, or while checking out, and the delivery address will be auto-filled. We have provisioned for a return URL in the login form so that we can redirect to that page on successful login.

Form Elements Don't Look the Same Across Browsers

While the XHTML code for forms is same for standard web and mobile web, the way form elements are rendered differs from browser to browser. Some browsers show the select drop down as a list of radio buttons, some show it like a menu. If you use `<optgroup>` in select options, some will render it as a nested menu.

Some browsers allow inline editing of text fields, some get into a full screen editing mode. Many render large text boxes. We have already seen how forms render in Openwave and Opera Mini. Check out the following screenshots of how the POTR homepage and login form are rendered in different browsers.

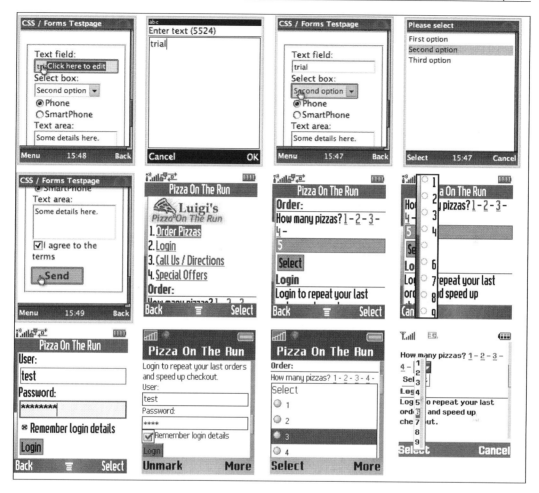

Here's a run down on the screenshots (from top left):

1. Opera Mini—test page—clicking to edit a text field

2. Opera Mini—test page—full screen text field editing

3. Opera Mini—test page—select drop down

4. Opera Mini—test page—full screen view of select options

5. Opera Mini—test page—text area, checkbox, and submit button activation

6. Motorola v3i—POTR homepage—navigation menu

7. Motorola v3i—POTR homepage—links, select drop down

8. Motorola v3i—POTR homepage—radio button style select drop down rendering

9. Motorola v3i—login form—inline text field editing

10. Sony Ericsson k750i—login form rendering

11. Sony Ericsson k750i—inline radio button style rendering of drop downs

12. Samsung Z105's rendering of select drop down & POTR homepage

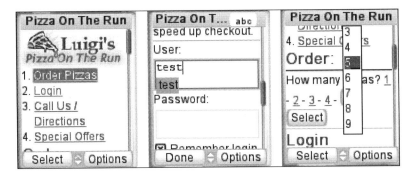

The screenshot above shows how Openwave browser renders the POTR homepage. It provides auto-completion by default on text fields, and you have to activate editing by pressing the softkey. Select drop downs are shown on the same screen.

The difference in form control rendering affects usability! Imagine a page with six drop downs to select starting and ending dates. This is normal for a web application, but will be very difficult for a mobile user. Radio buttons, checkboxes, and text boxes are preferred controls for mobile forms. Links that pass parameters via GET are even easier. Make sure you pick the right controls for your forms!

Form Processing Does not Change!

If you are overwhelmed by this, here's something that can bring you peace! Once the form is submitted to the server, you can process it the same way as you do it on standard web applications. Let's see the code that actually does the authentication in `login.inc.php` to prove this!

```php
<?php
if (isset($_POST["username"]) && isset($_POST["password"]) )
{
    $userObj = new User();
    if($userObj->Login($_POST["username"], $_POST["password"]))
    {
        if ($_POST["remember"] == "1")
        {
            setcookie("potrUsername", $_POST["username"
                                    ], time()+(30*24*3600));
```

```
        setcookie("potrPassword", $_POST["password"
                                       ], time()+(30*24*3600)));
    }
    $_SESSION["userId"] = $userObj->id;
    if (isset($_REQUEST["return"]))
    {
        header("Location: ".$_REQUEST["return"]);
    }
    else
    {
        include("profile.inc.php");
        return;
    }
}
else
{
    echo '<p class="error">Sorry, login failed. Please try again.</p>';
}
}
?>
```

Isn't this how you would process a standard web form? We first check if we got the username and password, and then let the User class handle the authentication. Once verified, we set a cookie if the user opted to remember the login details. We then redirect the user to a return URL if specified, or to the profile page. If we could not verify, we show an error message. This PHP code is placed before the login form XHTML code, so the username and password entered will be auto-filled if the login failed. That's all!

Handling Sessions and User Login

We made the homepage and login script and showed it to Luigi. Luigi pulled up his mobile browser and went ahead to log in. And then Murphy hit us! Luigi entered the correct username and password, it showed him the profile page, but if he moved to any other page, it would say he was not logged in! Murphy's law says that anything that can go wrong will go wrong, and at the worst possible time. That time is typically when your client is going to test the app. And then we learn!

Even though we are not using cookies for authentication, PHP uses a cookie to store the Session ID. Without that cookie, the session cannot be retrieved and a new session will be generated on each request. To our misfortune, not all mobile devices support cookies. And if they do, they also have restrictions on the maximum number of cookies or length of each cookie. There is a good enough reason behind this! Mobile devices have limited storage and processing capacity. A cookie stores data in text format at the client end. Cookies for a particular URL are sent with each request to that URL—which may not be feasible for a tiny browser. Most of today's mobile browsers support cookies, but some need a WAP gateway between the client and the server for cookies. The WAP gateway acts as a smart proxy—managing cookies and any other information for the client.

We have two alternatives to deal with this. One, to support only browsers that can accept cookies, and two, to remove the use of cookies in our application. Luigi does not want to eliminate any users, so wants us to handle user sessions on our own. (He never goes the easy way!)

Thankfully, we can still use PHP sessions. PHP works with session IDs stored in cookies or passed as a request parameter. By default, session IDs are stored in cookies. But we can pass them in the URLs to ensure our application works with browsers that do not support cookies.

If your server allows customizing PHP configuration, you can have PHP automatically insert session IDs in URLs and forms. Here's the magic piece of code that gives us full session support without needing the browser to support cookies. This code is written in a PHP file, but can be configured using the `php.ini` or `.htaccess` file as well. Most shared hosting environments would support this.

```
ini_set("session.use_trans_sid", 1);
ini_set("url_rewriter.tags", "a=href,area=href,input=src,fieldset=");
ini_set("arg_separator.output","&amp;");
session_start();
```

The first line enables transparent session ID support—a mighty PHP feature that can add session ID to the tags you specify. The second line defines the tags that will be rewritten to include session ID. For forms, we use the fieldset tag around form fields to pass session ID with POST data automatically.

The third line about argument separators tells PHP to use & as the argument separator in all links it generates. This configuration is essential to make your documents XHTML MP compliant. PHP uses only & by default, and that will break XHTML validation. The configuration affects only links that PHP will generate, and not the ones we code. So, we still have to use & in the links we make.

Thankfully, the trick worked. And Luigi is back to normal after we did this fix!

Handling Authentication can be Tricky

Managing sessions and cookies while working with mobile web browsers can be tricky. As a matter of fact, consistently managing authentication across different browsers has been very difficult for many people. We have covered this section in detail to make you aware of the issues you may face while building your own applications. We recommend testing across simulators and real devices to ensure that authentication works as expected in your applications.

Taking Orders

The core functionality of our system is to select pizzas and side dishes for an order. The first step is to select the number of pizzas to order. Next is to customize each pizza for size, crust, and toppings. We then let the user select side dishes and beverages. Next is to take the delivery address and confirm the order.

Take a look at the following figure. It shows how the Openwave browser displays the ordering process. You can then review the code that follows to learn how the pages are constructed.

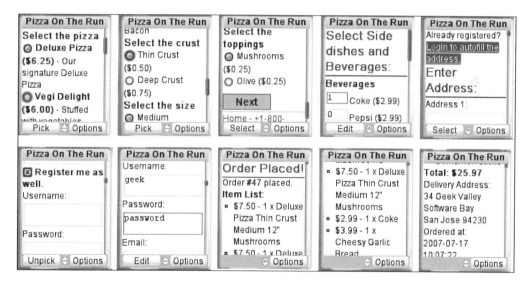

Here's the code for selecting pizzas.

```php
<?php
// Load all product and variation information.
// categoryId 1 is for pizzas. We also show them in order of
// popularity by sorting them on priority
```

```php
$prodObj = new Product();
$products = $prodObj->GetAll("categoryId = 1", "priority asc");
// Variation Type could be Size / Crust / Toppings
$varObj = new Variation();
$varObj = $varObj->GetAll("", "type asc");
// numPizza is the total number of pizzas to order,
// numPizzaDone is the number of already selected pizzas
$currentPizza = $_REQUEST["numPizzaDone"]+1;
echo '<h2>Customize Your Pizza #'.$currentPizza.':</h2>
<form action="index.php" method="POST"><fieldset>
<input type="hidden" name="action" value="order" />';
// If this is the last pizza, move to step 2 on submission
if ($currentPizza == $_REQUEST["numPizza"])
{
    $step = 2;
}
else
{
    $step = 1;
}
echo '<input type="hidden" name="step" value="'.$step.'" />';
echo '<input type="hidden" name="numPizza" value="'.$_
                                    REQUEST["numPizza"].'" />';
echo '<input type="hidden" name="numPizzaDone"
                            value="'.$currentPizza.'" />';
// Pass details of previously selected pizzas
if (is_array($_REQUEST["pizza"]))
{
    foreach ($_REQUEST["pizza"] as $key=>$prodId)
    {
        echo '<input type="hidden" name="pizza['.$key.']"
                            value="'.$prodId.'" />';
        foreach($_REQUEST["variation"][$key] as $variationKey=>$varId)
        {
        echo '<input type="hidden" name="variation['.$key.'][
                        '.$variationKey.']" value="'.$varId.'" />';
        }
    }
}
echo '<h3>Select the pizza</h3>';
// Select the first item by default, items are already
//                                  sorted by priority of display
$checked = 'checked="checked"';
foreach($products as $product)
```

```
{
    echo '<input type="radio" name="pizza['.$currentPizza.'
                        ]" value="'.$product["id"].'" '.$checked.'/>';
    echo '<strong>'.$product["name"].' ($'.$product["price"].'
                                            )</strong> - ';
    echo $product["description"].'<br />';
    $checked = '';
}
// Select the variations of this pizza now
$currentVariationType = "";
$currentVariation = -1;
foreach($varObj as $variation)
{
    if ($currentVariationType != $variation["type"])
    {
        $currentVariationType = $variation["type"];
        echo '<h3>Select the '.$currentVariationType.'</h3>';
        $currentVariation++;
        $checked = 'checked="checked"';
    }
    echo '<input type="radio" name="variation['.$currentPizza.'][
                        '.$currentVariation.']" value="'.$variation[
                                        "id"].'" '.$checked.'/>';
    echo $variation["name"].' ($'.$variation["price"].')<br />';
    $checked = '';
}
// Inputs done, Show appropriate next action label for button
echo '<input type="submit" name="option" value="';
if ($step == 2) echo 'Sidedishes and Beverages';
else echo 'Select Pizza #'.($currentPizza+1);
echo '" /></fieldset></form>';
?>
```

Here's how we select the side dishes and beverages.

```
<?php
// Load side dishes and category information
$prodObj = new Product();
$products = $prodObj->GetAll("categoryId > 1", "
                                    categoryId asc, priority asc");
$catObj = new Category();
$categories = $catObj->GetAll();

echo '<h2>Select Side dishes and Beverages:</h2>
<form action="index.php" method="POST"><fieldset>
<input type="hidden" name="action" value="order" />
```

```
<input type="hidden" name="step" value="3" />';
// Pass details of previously selected pizzas
if (is_array($_REQUEST["pizza"]))
{
    foreach ($_REQUEST["pizza"] as $key=>$prodId)
    {
        echo '<input type="hidden" name="pizza[
                        '.$key.']" value="'.$prodId.'" />';
        foreach($_REQUEST["variation"][$key] as $variationKey=>$varId)
        {
        echo '<input type="hidden" name="variation['.$key.'][
                    '.$variationKey.']" value="'.$varId.'" />';
        }
    }
}
$lastCategoryId = 0;
foreach($products as $info)
{
    // Show a menu category heading at start
    if ($info["categoryId"] != $lastCategoryId)
    {
        echo '<a name="'.$categories[$info["categoryId"]][
                                            "category"].'" />
            <h3>'.$categories[$info["categoryId"]]["category"].'</h3>';
        $lastCategoryId = $info["categoryId"];
    }
    // If priority is high, default to 1 quantity for the item, else 0
    $value = $info['priority'] < 3 ? 1 : 0;
    echo '<input name="sideItems['.$info['id'].']" type=
            "text" value="'.$value.'" size="3" maxLength="2" style=
            "-wap-input-format: \'2N\'; -wap-input-required: true"/
                >'.$info['name'].' ($'.$info['price'].') <br />';
}
echo '<input type="submit" name="option" value="Enter Address" />
                                        </fieldset></form>';

?>
```

Constraining User Input with WCSS

While entering the quantity of side dishes and beverages, we used a style to
constrain the user input.

```
style="-wap-input-format: \'2N\'; -wap-input-required: true"
```

The `-wap-input-format` style defines what can be entered into the field. In this case,
we allow up to two numeric characters.

`-wap-input-required` sets whether the field is required or not. Not all browsers support these properties consistently. But it's good practice to provide such constraints at the user side in addition to server-side validation. Supporting mobile browsers will change the input mode to numeric mode (or other) automatically based on the input mask. This makes it very convenient for the user as she or he does not have to keep changing input modes among form fields. The next two figures show this CSS in effect in the Openwave browser.

`-wap-input-format` takes a format string as its value. This value becomes the input mask for the field. The following table shows valid format characters.

Character	Meaning
a	Any lowercase letter or symbol.
A	Any uppercase letter or symbol.
n	Any numeric or symbolic character.
N	Any numeric character.
x	Any lowercase letter, numeric, or symbolic character.
X	Any uppercase letter, numeric, or symbolic character.
m	Any character. Browser input mode is set to lowercase by default.
M	Any character. Browser input mode is set to uppercase by default.
*	Wildcard: Zero or more characters of selected format. E.g. *x
2 (some number)	Wildcard: Up to 2 (or the number) characters of the selected format. E.g. 2N, 10m.

You can apply this formatting only to text, password, and textarea fields. Here are some examples of typical usage (and wrong usage).

Input Mask	Meaning
NNNNN	5 numeric characters. E.g. Zip code.
10a	Up to 10 lowercase characters. E.g. Username/password.
100m	Up to 100 characters, input mode set to lowercase by default.
A*m	First letter capital, then any number of characters. E.g. Name.
2N2N	Wrong! You can use the wildcard character only once in the input mask.
A*aa	Wrong! The wildcard format must be at the end of the mask. Correct use is A*a.

If an invalid mask is assigned to `-wap-input-format`, the browser will ignore the mask. You can include escaped characters in the input mask—put two backslashes before the character to escape it. If the `-wap-input-format` and `-wap-input-required` styles conflict with each other, `-wap-input-required` will have precedence. So if your input mask is "N" (meaning one numeric character is required) but `-wap-input-required` is set to false, empty input is OK for the field.

On POTR, once the side dishes are selected, we take the delivery address. We use CSS classes to constrain the input for address fields, zip, and phone. Here's an example:

```
<style>
/* This should be in the CSS file for maximum compatibility */
.zip {
-wap-input-required: true;
-wap-input-format: "NNNNN"
}
</style>
Zip: <input type="text" name="zip" class="zip" value="<?php echo
$data["zip"]; ?>"/>
```

Single-Step Registration and Order Placement on POTR

In the checkout process, we also allow the user to login so that the address can be pulled from the registration information. If the user is not registered, she or he can tick a checkbox to register with the entered address. The following code shows how we register the user during checkout. Most of the work is done by two methods provided in the BaseModel—`PopulateFromArray()` and `Save()`.

```
<?php
// Save the order and register the user if opted for
```

```php
if ($_REQUEST["toRegister"] == 1)
{
    // Register the user
    $userObj = new User();
    $userObj->PopulateFromArray($_POST);
    if ($userObj->Save())
    {
        $msg = "Registered successfully.";
        $_SESSION["userId"] = $userObj->id;
    }
    else
    {
        echo '<p class="error">Could not register. Please
                                            try again.</p>';
        $data = $_REQUEST;
        // Include the address collection /
        //                              registration info page again
        include("order_step3.inc.php");
        return;
    }
}
?>
```

If everything is alright, we can go ahead and insert complete order details in the database. The following code illustrates how we do this.

```php
<?php
// We pass the products & variations objects to the order to refer to
// product pricing and names. Are needed for total calculation and
// order printing. The $orderDetail array contains the
//                                          delivery address,
// userId, order time and order status
$orderObj = new Order($products, $variations, "orders", $orderDetail);
// If there are no selected items, can't proceed
if (!is_array($_SESSION["orderInfo"]["pizza"]))
{
    echo '<p class="error">Did not find any pizzas to
                                order. Please select again!</p>';
    return;
}
// Add pizzas to the order
foreach ($_SESSION["orderInfo"]["pizza"] as $key=>$prodId)
{
    $itemData = array();
    $varData = array();
```

```
    $itemData["productId"] = $prodId;
    $itemData["orderId"] = 0;
    foreach($_SESSION["orderInfo"]["variation"][
                                $key] as $variationKey=>$varId)
    {
        $varData[]["variationId"] = $varId;
        $varData[]["orderItemId"] = 0;
    }
    // This will add orderItem and orderItemVariation
    $orderObj->addItem($itemData, $varData);
}
// Add Side dishes
foreach ($_SESSION["orderInfo"]["sideItems"] as $prodId=>$qty)
{
    $itemData = array();
    $itemData["productId"] = $prodId;
    $itemData["quantity"] = $qty;
    $itemData["orderId"] = 0;
    if ($qty > 0)
    {
    $orderObj->addItem($itemData);
    }
}
// Save the order, and notify the user
// The Order class saves data to orders, orderItems and
//                                          orderItemVariations
// tables. It also has a __toString() method which gives
//                                          an HTML formatted
// output of the full order
if ($orderObj->Save())
{
    echo "<h2>Order Placed!</h2>";
    echo $orderObj;
    echo "<p>Your order will soon be on its way. Payment
                                        on delivery.</p>";
    $_SESSION["orderInfo"] = null;
}
else
{
    echo "<p>Sorry, the order could not be placed. Please
                                        try again.</p>";

}
?>
```

That completes the ordering process! Luigi and his team will now make some delicious pizzas and deliver them in a few minutes!

Special Effects with CSS

Luigi wants to run discount offers on the mobile store. He also wants to display the offers with some special effects! Since we can't be sure about how many people will have Flash support in their mobile browsers, we need to do something simpler. We can use animated GIFs to draw attention. But WCSS can do a few tricks that will come to our rescue! We can slide some content and show it like a marquee. That should make Luigi happy!

Here's the style sheet and XHTML code for creating a marquee.

```
<style>
/* This should be in the CSS file */
.offer {
    display: -wap-marquee;
    -wap-marquee-dir: rtl;
    -wap-marquee-style: slide;
    -wap-marquee-loop: 5;
    -wap-marquee-speed: slow
}
</style>
<div class="offer">
<img src="assets/pep_spice_offer.jpg" alt="Pepperoni Spice at
                                just $7!" width="200" height="100" />
</div>
```

The style definition should be in a CSS file for maximum compatibility. The style properties themselves are self-explanatory! The mandatory property to create a marquee is `"display: -wap-marquee"`. Applying that style to any element will slide it from right to left at normal speed once. The following figure shows the marquee in a Nokia browser.

Use marquees with caution! We wouldn't advise Luigi to use this more than once on the site! Use a marquee to draw attention, but ensure it does not go on too long to bore or distract the user. We don't want people to get busy looking at animations! We want them to order pizzas!

Luigi's Pizza On The Run is Live!

After many nights with XHTML, WCSS, PHP, and a dozen assorted pizzas, Luigi's POTR can go live now. The ordering process is in place. Users can register and auto-fill address after logging in. The menu is in place and we can show high-selling items at the top by setting priorities. We haven't done the code to repeat orders yet, but that can wait for a future version!

Luigi took a test drive of POTR and was thrilled. He especially liked how an order can be placed without much thinking! Orders make him happy!

There are a few glitches though. The site does not look perfect on all the browsers. We need to do something to adapt content according to different browsers. Luigi has also asked for a feature to show pizza images on phones with larger screens. Friends who started using the app have requested SMS features as well. Let's bunch them all up, and implement them in the next few chapters!

Summary

We did so much! We learned fundamentals of designing mobile web applications. And we created a solid Pizza On The Run application. Specifically, we learned:

- Mobile devices come in variety of screen sizes. Selecting the right size for development depends on the target devices.

- Newer devices have larger screens and good small screen rendering techniques. Normal sites too display well on them. Yet, the majority of devices can't do this. It makes sense to develop a mobile-specific version of your application.

- Web layouts don't work on mobile browsers—we need to show things in vertical blocks.

- Wireless CSS is similar to standard CSS and perfect to manage the design of mobile websites.

- CSS and forms render differently on different browsers.

- We also designed the Classes, Database schema, and Coding Framework for POTR.

- Ordered list is useful for navigation; the accesskey attribute allows quick activation of links.

- Form handling on the server does not change!

- Handling sessions and user login requires understanding the target browsers and the server-side programming technology.

- We also implemented a mobile-friendly ordering process for POTR.

- We can constrain user input with WCSS.

- WCSS can also be used to show simple marquee animations.

In the next chapter, we will see how we can adapt our site to different mobile devices. Get yourself a pizza till then!

4
Adapting to User Devices

Luigi's Pizza On The Run mobile shop is working well now. And he wants to adapt it to different mobile devices. Let us learn that in this chapter! And specifically, let's look at:

- Understanding the Lowest Common Denominator method
- Finding and comparing features of different mobile devices
- Deciding to adapt or not.
- Adapting and progressively enhancing POTR application using Wireless Abstraction Library
- Detecting device capabilities
- Evaluating tools that can aid in adaptation
- Moving your blog to the mobile web

By the end of this chapter, you will have a strong foundation in adapting to different devices.

What is Adaptation?

As we discussed in Chapter 1, adaptation, sometimes called multiserving, means delivering content as per each user device's capabilities. If the visiting device is an old phone supporting only WML, you will show a WML page with Wireless Bitmap (wbmp) images. If it is a newer XHTML MP-compliant device, you will deliver an XHTML MP version, customized according to the screen size of the device. If the user is on iMode in Japan, you will show a Compact HTML (cHTML) version that's more forgiving than XHTML. This way, users get the best experience possible on their device.

Do I Need Adaptation?

I am sure most of you are wondering why you would want to create so many different versions of your mobile site? Isn't following the XHTML MP standard enough?

On the Web, you could make sure that you followed XHTML and the site will work in all browsers. The browser-specific quirks are limited and fixes are easy. However, in the mobile world, you have thousands of devices using hundreds of different browsers.

You need adaptation precisely for that reason! If you want to serve all users well, you need to worry about adaptation. WML devices will give up if they encounter a `<b>` tag within an `<a>` tag. Some XHTML MP browsers will not be able to process a form if it is within a table. But a table within a form will work just fine. If your target audience is limited, and you know that they are going to use a limited range of browsers, you can live without adaptation.

Can't I just Use Common Capabilities and Ignore the Rest?

You can. Finding the Lowest Common Denominator (LCD) of the capabilities of target devices, you can design a site that will work reasonably well in all devices. Devices with better capabilities than LCD will see a version that may not be very beautiful but things will work just as well.

As a matter of fact, this is what we did in the last chapter. We decided to support only XHTML MP devices. To render across all screen sizes and handle sessions on our own, we decided to keep the page size down and use only basic WCSS. Most people take this approach because it's easier and faster. In Chapter 1, we saw the capabilities W3C has listed as the Default Delivery Context—or the minimum expected features. We can use that as our LCD and design our mobile site.

How to Determine the LCD?

If you are looking for something more than the W3C DDC guidelines, you may be interested in finding out the capabilities of different devices to decide on your own what features you want to use in your application. There is a nice tool that allows you to search on device capabilities and compare them side by side. Take a look at the following screenshot showing mDevInf (`http://mdevinf.sourceforge.net/`) in action, showing image formats supported on a generic iMode device.

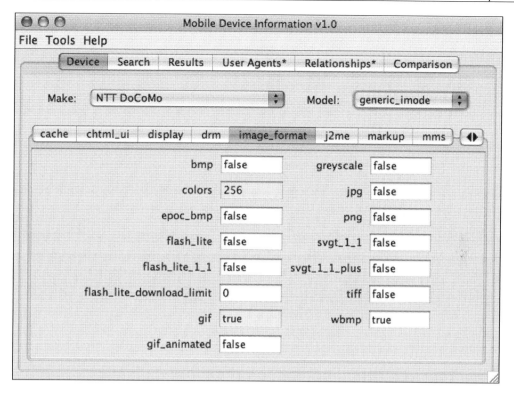

You can search for devices and compare them, and then come to a conclusion about features you want to use.

This is all good. But when you want to cater to wider mobile audience, you must consider adaptation. You don't want to fight with browser quirks and silly compatibility issues. You want to focus on delivering a good solution. Adaptation can help you there.

OK, So How do I Adapt?

You have three options to adapt:

1. Design alternative CSS: this will control the display of elements and images. This is the easiest method. You can detect the device and link an appropriate CSS file.

2. Create multiple versions of pages: redirect the user to a device-specific version. This is called "alteration". This way you get the most control over what is shown to each device.

3. Automatic Adaptation: create content in one format and use a tool to generate device-specific versions. This is the most elegant method.

Let us rebuild the pizza selection page on POTR to learn how we can detect the device and implement automatic adaptation.

Fancy Pizza Selection

Luigi has been asking to put up photographs of his delicious pizzas on the mobile site, but we didn't do that so far to save bandwidth for users. Let us now go ahead and add images to the pizza selection page. We want to show larger images to devices that can support them.

Remember the XHTML to invoke a phone call? The two approaches of using wtai and tel? Some customers have complained that they were not able to make a call using that link. The cause is that their browsers did not understand the tel link. Let us adapt that so that the user gets the markup her or his browser can understand!

Review the code shown below. It's an abridged version of the actual code.

```php
<?php
include_once("wall_prepend.php");
?>
<wall:document><wall:xmlpidtd />
  <wall:head>
    <wall:title>Pizza On The Run</wall:title>
    <link href="assets/mobile.css" type="text/css" rel="stylesheet" />
  </wall:head>
  <wall:body>
<?php
echo '<wall:h2>Customize Your Pizza #'.$currentPizza.':</wall:h2>';
<wall:form enable_wml="false" action="index.php" method="POST">
<fieldset>
<wall:input type="hidden" name="action" value="order" />';
// If we did not get the total number of pizzas to order,
//                                         let the user select
if ($_REQUEST["numPizza"] == -1)
{
    echo 'Pizzas to Order: <wall:select name="numPizza">';
    for($i=1; $i<=9; $i++)
    {
        echo '<wall:option value="'.$i.'">'.$i.'</wall:option>';
    }
    echo '</wall:select><wall:br/>';
}
else
{
```

```
        echo '<wall:input type="hidden" name="numPizza" value="'.$_
REQUEST["numPizza"].'" />';
    }
    echo '<wall:h3>Select the pizza</wall:h3>';
    // Select the pizza
    $checked = 'checked="checked"';
    foreach($products as $product)
    {
        // Show a product image based on the device size
        echo '<wall:img src="assets/pizza_'.$product[
                        "id"].'_120x80.jpg" alt="'.$product["name"].'">
        <wall:alternate_img src="assets/pizza_'.$product[
                        "id"].'_300x200.jpg" test="'.($wall->getCapa(
                                'resolution_width') >= 200).'" />
        <wall:alternate_img nopicture="true" test="'.(
                                !$wall->getCapa('jpg')).'" />
        </wall:img><wall:br />';
        echo '<wall:input type="radio" name="pizza[
            '.$currentPizza.']" value="'.$product["id"].'" '.$checked.'/>';
        echo '<strong>'.$product["name"].' ($'.$product[
                                        "price"].')</strong> - ';
        echo $product["description"].'<wall:br/>';
        $checked = '';
    }
    echo '<wall:input type="submit" class="button" name=
                                        "option" value="Next" />
</fieldset></wall:form>';
?>
    <p><wall:a href="?action=home">Home</wall:a> - <wall:caller
tel="+18007687669">+1-800-POTRNOW</wall:caller></p>
    </wall:body>
</wall:html>
```

What are Those <wall:*> Tags?

All those <wall:*> tags are at the heart of adaptation. Wireless Abstraction Library (WALL) is an open-source tag library that transforms the WALL tags into WML, XHTML, or cHTML code. E.g. iMode devices use <br> tag and simply ignore <br />. WALL will ensure that cHTML devices get a <br> tag and XHTML devices get <br />. You can find a very good tutorial and extensive reference material on WALL from: http://wurfl.sourceforge.net/java/wall.php. You can download WALL and many other tools too from that site.

WALL4PHP—a PHP port of WALL is available from http://wall.laacz.lv/. That's what we are using for POTR.

Let's Make Sense of This Code!

What are the critical elements of this code? Most of it is very similar to standard XHTML MP. The biggest difference is that tags have a "`wall:`" prefix. Let us look at some important pieces:

- The `wall_prepend.php` file at the beginning loads the WALL class, detects the user's browser, and loads its capabilities. You can use the `$wall` object in your code later to check device capabilities etc.

- `<wall:document>` tells the WALL parser to start the document code. `<wall: xmlpidtd />` will insert the XHTML/WML/CHTML prolog as required. This solves part of the headache in adaptation.

- The next few lines define the page title and meta tags. Code that is not in `<wall:*>` tags is sent to the browser as is.

- The heading tag will render as a bold text on a WML device. You can use many standard tags with WALL. Just prefix them with "`wall:`".

- We do not want to enable WML support in the form. It requires a few more changes in the document structure, and we don't want it to get complex for this example! If you want to support forms on WML devices, you can enable it in the `<wall:form>` tag.

- The `img` and `alternate_img` tags are a cool feature of WALL. You can specify the default image in the `img` tag, and then specify alternative images based on any condition you like. One of these images will be picked up at run time. WALL can even skip displaying the image all together if the `nopicture` test evaluates to true. In our code, we show a 120x100 pixels images by default, and show a larger image if the device resolution is more than 200 pixels. As the image is a JPG, we skip showing the image if the device cannot support JPG images. The `alternate_img` tag also supports showing some icons available natively on the phone. You can refer to the WALL reference for more on this.

- Adapting the phone call link is dead simple. Just use the `<wall:caller>` tag. Specify the number to call in the `tel` attribute, and you are done. You can also specify what to display if the phone does not support phone links in `alt` attribute.

When you load the URL in your browser, WALL will do all the heavy lifting and show a mouth-watering pizza—a larger mouth-watering pizza if you have a large screen!

Can I Use All XHTML Tags?

WALL supports many XHTML tags. It has some additional tags to ease menu display and invoke phone calls. You can use `<wall:block>` instead of `<p>` or `<div>` tags because it will degrade well, and yet allow you to specify CSS `class` and `id`. WALL does not have tags for tables, though it can use tables to generate menus. Here's a list of WALL tags you can use:

> *a, alternate_img, b, block, body, br, caller, cell, cool_menu, cool_menu_css, document, font, form, h1, h2, h3, h4, h5, h6, head, hr, i, img, input, load_capabilities, marquee, menu, menu_css, option, select, title, wurfl_device_id, xmlpidtd.*

Complete listings of the attributes available with each tag, and their meanings are available from: `http://wurfl.sourceforge.net/java/refguide.php`.

Will This Work Well for WML?

WALL can generate WML. WML itself has limited capabilities so you will be restricted in the markup that you can use. You have to enclose content in <wall: block> tags and test rigorously to ensure full WML support. WML handles user input in a different way and we can't use radio buttons or checkboxes in forms. A workaround is to change radio buttons to a menu and pass values using the GET method. Another is to convert them to a select drop down. We are not building WML capability in POTR yet.

WALL is still useful for us as it can support cHTML devices and will automatically take care of XHTML implementation variations in different browsers. It can even generate some cool menus for us! Take a look at the following screenshot.

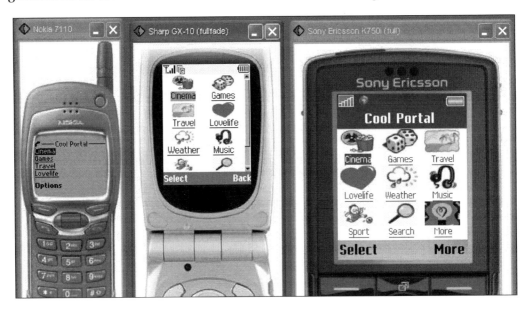

Device Detection and Capabilities

We looked at what WALL can do and how easy it is to implement it. But how does it do that? WALL, and many other open-source (and commercial) tools use WURFL—Wireless Universal Resource File. The mDevInf tool that we saw earlier in this chapter is entirely based on WURFL. WURFL is a massive XML file, listing capabilities of all known mobile devices (almost!). It is actively maintained and also derives information from UAProf—another standard for managing device capabilities.

At the heart of any device detection is the User Agent header sent by the browser. All device detection techniques check the User Agent ($_SERVER['HTTP_USER_AGENT'] variable for PHP) and look up their database to find the characteristics of that device.

Here are some of the things WURFL can tell you about a device:

- Screen size of the device

- Supported image, audio, video, ringtone, wallpaper, and screensaver formats

- Whether the device supports Unicode

- Is it a wireless device? What markup does it support?

- What XHTML MP/WML/cHTML features does it support? Does it work with tables? Can it work with standard HTML?

- Does it have a pointing device? Can it use CSS?

- Does it have Flash Lite/J2ME support? What features?

- Can images be used as links on this device? Can it display image and text on the same line?

- If this is an iMode phone, what region is it from? Japan? US? Europe?

- Does the device auto-expand a select drop down? Does it have inline input for text fields?

- What SMS/MMS features are supported?

The list goes on. But you can make some intelligent decisions in your application based on the device now. You can even conditionally print `<wall>` tags. E.g. show a download link only if the device has download support.

WURFL API is available in many programming languages, including Java, PHP, .Net, Ruby, and Python. You can download it from: http://wurfl.sourceforge.net/.

XML Processing can Bog Down My Server, is There Something Easier?

Yes! The WURFL XML file is above 4MB, and despite many structural optimizations, processing it on every request will certainly slow down your server. Many APIs provide caching to speed things up. But having this available in a database will be best. Tera-WURFL is a PHP package that uses MySQL to store WURFL data. It bundles WALL and an admin panel—making it the top choice for mobile web adaptation.

Setting up Tera WURFL involves downloading the latest package from http://www.tera-wurfl.com/, extracting the files and entering the database connection information in the configuration file. It will load up the device data to the database and can start serving WALL pages.

What About W3C's DIAL?

W3C's DIAL (Device Independent Authoring Language) is a combination of XHTML 2, XForms, and DISelect. DIAL (`http://www.w3.org/TR/dial/`) was created to develop a language that will allow consistent delivery across devices and contexts. Though the language is new, it's getting a good response and is something to keep track of!

Other Useful Tools for Adaptation

Adapting a site for different devices goes beyond markup generation. Commercial tools such as Changing Worlds, Dynetic, and Volantis do a good comprehensive job in adaptation. Let us look at some more interesting open-source tools in this area.

Dynamically Resizing Images

If we can generate markup code dynamically, we might as well resize images dynamically! Maybe we can detect the screen size using WURFL and write logic that will resize a large image to fit the device screen. This will increase the load on the server a little bit as we resize the image, but we can save the image to disk for later usage and manage the additional load. This will cut down on the chore of resizing images for different resolutions every time we add one.

There are a few ready libraries that work with WURFL and can resize images and even change their format.

GAIA Image Transcoder (`http://wurfl.sourceforge.net/utilities/gaia.php`) is one such tool in Java. It even lets you define regions of interest to help in preview and place on the image.

PHP Image Rendering Library (`http://wurfl.sourceforge.net/utilities/phpimagerendering.php`) is another implementation in PHP.

Image Server (`http://wurfl.sourceforge.net/utilities/imageserver.php`) can work as a filter for your Java server, optimizing images without a trace of what's happening to the user!

Quick and Easy Way to Make Your Blog Mobile

If the job at hand is to make a mobile web version of a blog, you can do it in a matter of minutes! FeedBurner (`http://www.feedburner.com`) and Feed2Mobile (`http://feed2mobile.kaywa.com/`) take the RSS feed from your blog and show it in a mobile-friendly manner. Users just point to the new URL and they can access your mobile blog!

If you want full control, and want to set up something on your blog itself, head for Mobile Web Toolkit (`http://www.beeweb.com`). MWT's WordPress plug-in can get your blog mobile within 10 minutes. MWT allows you to customize what widgets show up to users of different browsers in a friendly AJAX editor. Plug-ins for other content management systems are on their way. MWT is a very interesting concept and advocates delivering a rich experience to mobile users, rather than restricting them with some lowest common denominator design.

On the other hand, many content management systems have now started supporting versions adapted to mobile devices. By the time this book goes to print, all major CMS will have mobile web support.

MyMobileWeb: Going the Semantic Way

MyMobileWeb (`http://forge.morfeo-project.org/`) is a Java-based open-source tool to build .mobi-compliant websites. It is a comprehensive framework that uses declarative XML to build the presentation layer (very similar to WALL) and an MVC architecture for handling various events.

MyMobileWeb is an ambitious project. The team is working on semantic mobile web, context awareness and mobile AJAX. Some of the features that may interest you:

- It does not do markup transcoding at run time, but generates device-specific pages at publish time. This gives better performance.

- The visual controls are defined through a declarative language and can interoperate with JSTL for dynamism. They are also rendered based on the context or rules that we can specify.

- The framework comes with ready visual controls for layouts, date control, RSS etc. It can even do binding of visual controls with data, and can generate a grid to display data and paginate.

- You get control over the visual aspects—CSS, alternatine content, hiding pages based on device, etc.

- It has a validation framework that can work on both client side and server side depending on scripting support at the client.

- Comes with an Eclipse plug-in!

HAWHAW: As Simple as a Laugh?

HAWHAW (`http://www.hawhaw.de/`) has a funny acronym, but is a great idea. It stands for HTML And WML Hybrid Adapted Webserver. HAWHAW is an open-source script written in PHP. You can create HAWHAW pages via PHP or XML. But the interesting thing about it is that it can even generate VoiceXML output. So not only can you build your standard and mobile website with it, you can even have people call in a number and do a complete interactive voice response system. You can even get some ideas from the HAWHAW implementation and build something of your own.

Summary

In this quick chapter, we learned when to adapt and how to adapt our mobile site to different devices. Specifically:

- We learned about the Lowest Common Denominator method, finding and comparing features of different mobile devices and deciding to adapt or not.

- We extended the Pizza On The Run application to adaptively display content using Wireless Abstraction Library.

- We saw how adaptation works in different browsers.

- We learned about WURFL and how it can be used to adapt based on browser capabilities.

- We reviewed tools that can aid in adaptation—Tera WURFL, MyMobileWeb, Mobile Web Toolkit, Image Server, GAIA Image Transcoder, and HAWHAW.

One note of caution! Do not over-constrain the content. Users expect the same kind of experience on the mobile that they have on the Web. As mobile web developers, we must strive to bridge the gap, not widen it.

In the next chapter, we will review the best practices of mobile web development: the standards and the opinions!

5

Developing Standards-Compliant Sites

The variety of device capabilities is one of the biggest constraints in mobile web development. In this chapter, we will learn about developing standards-compliant sites and in the process learn essential tricks in delivering the best experience to the users.

We will specifically look at:

- Running the ready.mobi test on your site
- Creating the structure, design, markup, and navigation for best user experience
- Collecting user behavior data to keep enhancing the site

After the adaptation work we did in the last chapter, Luigi is ready to roll out the Pizza On The Run mobile site to a wider audience. He's got ideas for making POTR more interactive (Web 2.0 style) and utilizing phone capabilities. But before we can do all that, we need to ensure that our site follows the best practices of mobile web development.

So let's go ahead and get POTR to the pit!

Running the ready.mobi Test

We could learn all the standards and best practices before we start development. But what's the fun in success if there were no failures behind it? So, how can we find out how badly (or well) we are doing in terms of mobile web best practices? Simple! Run the ready.mobi test on it! Ready.mobi is an online service that can review your mobile website and give feedback on a variety of aspects—XHTML, images, download sizes, etc. Let's see how our current site does on the ready.mobi test!

Time for Action: Test Your Site's Mobile Readiness with the ready.mobi Test

1. Upload your site to a server, so that it can be accessed using a public URL.

2. Access it from your browser/emulator to ensure the site loads and works without any errors.

3. Open `http://ready.mobi/` in your browser. Enter your site address in the form and submit.

4. On the next page, you will see the ready.mobi report as shown in the following screenshot.

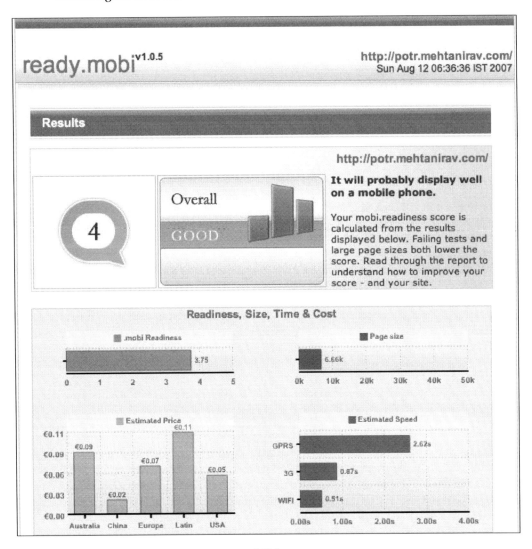

5. Check the overall readiness score as well as the speed test results. You can also review how your page will look on devices in the Visualization section. Take a look at the next screenshot, that demonstrates this.

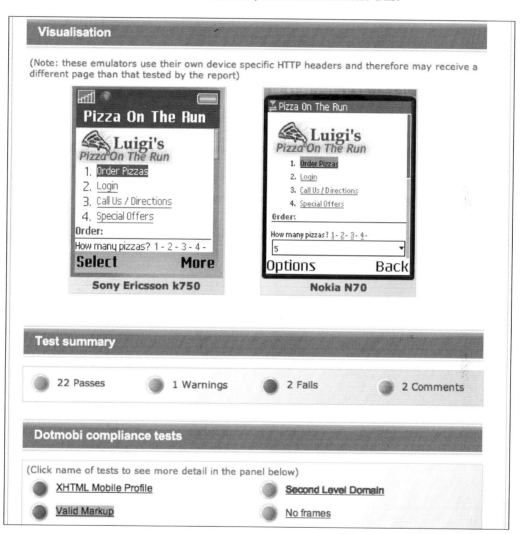

6. Check if you have any fails—indicated by red marks. If you have no red signs, go ahead, make your site live. Don't forget to tell all your friends about your latest venture! On the other hand, if you do have fails, you may want to fix them before going live!

7. We have two fails, resulting from the "name" attribute on <a> in our code, because the name attribute is not supported by the XHTML MP DTD we are using. The following screenshot shows the note about compliance test failure. This is a common mistake that we talked about in an earlier chapter. The solution is to use "id" attribute instead of "name" for identifying the anchors.

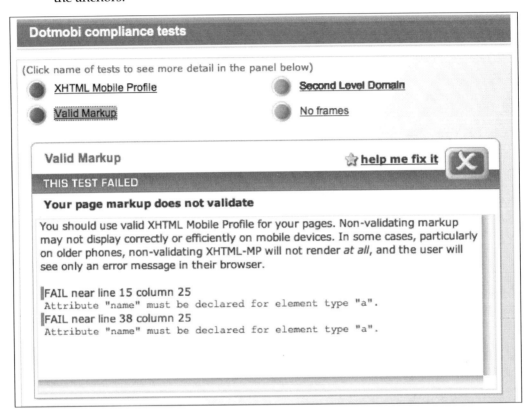

So What is Happening?

This is a comprehensive test that validates the page at the URL you entered. It validates against the XHTML MP standard, and .mobi's best practices of mobile web development. ready.mobi is an excellent tool to check how much time your page will take to load, whether it will render well across different browsers, and even whether it is semantically well constructed for mobile users.

 You can validate only one page with ready.mobi. So you will have to enter page addresses one by one to test your whole site.

Click inside one of the emulators to give focus to them. Now, navigate your site using just the keyboard. This will give you a good idea of how most mobile users will be accessing your site.

The following screenshot shows a list of tests ready.mobi runs apart from the standards-compliance tests. In the report, clicking on any item will open up notes about that test. This is a great way to explore and learn the best practices of mobile web development.

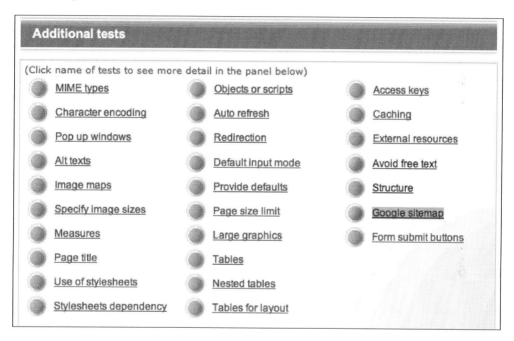

Now that we know how to run this test, let us review recommendations and best practices of mobile web development.

Creating the Structure, Design, Markup, and Navigation for Best User Experience

Learning XHTML and developing mobile sites is not that difficult. The real problems come when you want to ensure that the site works well across different devices. Adaptation certainly helps in the process, but if you know the pitfalls, your ride can be smoother.

There are a few notable efforts in the mobile web space that come up with best practices and recommendations.

- W3C Mobile Web Best Practices Basic Guidelines (`http://www.w3.org/TR/mobile-bp/`)
- Luca Passani's Global Authoring Practices (`http://www.passani.it/gap/`)
- OpenWave's Guidelines about XHTML Design (`http://developer.openwave.com/dvl/support/documentation/guides_and_references/best_practices_in_xhtml_design/index.htm`)
- Opera's Making Small Devices Look Great (See `http://my.opera.com/community/dev/device/`)

You should go through the best practices above for a deeper understanding of the rationale behind each recommendation. For this chapter, we have developed checklists you can use on your projects. These checklists come from the recommendations above as well as our experience in developing mobile and web applications.

Mobile Web Development Checklists

You can create your own version of these checklists, print them, and review them on your mobile web projects. Just keep checking off what's done, and understand what more can be done. The checklists are grouped by sections for easy reference.

Strategy

- Why mobile?
- Target users identified
- User goals defined, and task oriented
- Short URL for the homepage. No www. Maybe new subdomain
- User browser detection and delivering appropriate content
- Consistent delivery across devices
- Can something still be taken out of the page? Stay lean!

Testing Setup

- Testing in web browser
- Testing with 5 device emulators
- Testing with 2 real devices
- Testing with real users

Structure and Page Information

- Uses correct encoding—UTF-8 by default
- Sends correct XHTML doctype
- No frames, no pop-ups
- Page redirects on the server side, unless application needs it
- Short yet descriptive title for all pages
- Is the page structure understandable? Flows naturally?
- Minimum external resources (CSS, images, etc.)

Design and CSS

- Target resolution?
- Is high color contrast maintained?
- Usable with background images off?
- No tables, unless device support is guaranteed
- No nested tables, no tables for layout
- Textual representation of all non text elements (images, media, etc.)
- No pixel-based designs, use relative measures like em
- CSS for design
- No extraneous CSS code
- Font agnostic design
- Works with CSS off
- Uses lists for structure—ol, ul, dl
- Small icons are good, used where needed
- Consistent color theme across the site
- No wasted vertical space
- Uses blocks for page elements
- Background color to distinguish different blocks
- Unimportant text in gray color

Images

- No images without `alt` tag
- Tested with images turned off
- Image size according to device size
- Image size specified in XHTML
- Image resizing on the server, not at client
- No spacer images
- No image maps

Navigation and Links

- Shortest click-stream possible for each task
- No navigation bar in the header
- Check: is breadcrumb navigation adding value? Really?
- Most important links at the top
- Home, Contact, and few more important links in footer
- `accesskey` for important links in the page
- No more than 10 links on a page
- Clear, action-oriented label on each link
- Hide links to unsupported document types
- Site search in footer if needed
- Google sitemap present
- Links are search-engine friendly—avoid GET parameters via ? and &

Content

- Maximum 5 scrolls long
- No splash pages
- No stub pages without actual content or with links only
- Important content at top
- Clear and concise language for content
- Error messages, in the same language as content
- No unrelated content—check: will the user want it?
- Scrolls in one direction only, unless application needs secondary scroll

Markup

- Is the markup valid?
- No redundant markup; must be tidy
- Total page size (including markup, images, CSS) less than 20K
- XHTML is semantic, e.g. no h2 before h1
- Uses XHTML code for formatting, aided by CSS
- Minimal form elements, especially select boxes

User Input

- Avoids free text entry where possible
- Default selections/values as much as possible
- Default input mode, format, and language for fields
- Password field as input type="text", not input type="password", unless high security is needed

Objects, Security, Caching, Etc.

- No scripting without device detection + alternative
- No embedded objects without device detection + alternative
- Works without cookies
- `Cache-Control` header as per application need
- Pass session ID in URL
- Not mandatory to log in to see content, unless application requires so
- Phone numbers are linked to invoke call

Best Practices should be Upgraded!

When you develop your applications, you may keep the target devices and target users above the best practice recommendations. Best Practices are opinions and you will see arguments for and against some of the controversial items. You can come up with your own rules thumb of and tricks. Start with the items here, try them out on your projects, and keep evolving them.

Most Good Styles of Design and Software will Work on the Mobile Web Too

The mobile web is just another platform of delivering information. All good usability practices, graphic design patterns, and software development practices you have learned so far are still applicable to the mobile web. They are actually a base that you build your mobile development patterns on.

What's most important for any application is that it serves user needs. We may develop a mobile website, but the users may find it very difficult to use it. We can wait for them to send us complaints or be proactive and try to find out if they are having problems.

Luigi is very sensitive about his customers, so he wants to find out if they are having any troubles. So after applying all the best practices, we still want to put in place a routine to track user behavior and provide an opportunity to them to give us feedback. Let us see how we can do this.

Collecting User Behavior Data

We could follow all the best practices of mobile development. But what if we become proactive and try to understand how the user uses our application? If we track the pages our users are visiting, and how much time they are spending on each, we can get a fair sense of how the application is working for them. If we also track the browser data and some other application parameters, we will get a reasonably good picture of what's working and what's not working. If we find out that most of our users do not go past the first page in the ordering process, we know there is something wrong. We need to simplify the workflow.

Collecting user behavior data can allow us to generate intelligence out of the data. It will help us evolve our best practices and increase user satisfaction. Now we can use the web server logs for tracking page views. But we get full flexibility with our own tracking system. How can we set up a simple tracking system for POTR? The job is very easy for us because we have a centralized architecture. Let's see how we can do it.

Time for Action: Implementing User Tracking

1. Create a new table in the database. The following code shows the schema. You may use phpMyAdmin or any other database administration tool to do this.

```
CREATE TABLE `trackingdata` (
  `id` int(10) unsigned NOT NULL auto_increment,
  `userId` int(10) unsigned NOT NULL,
```

```
`sessionId` varchar(40)  NOT NULL,
`accessTime` timestamp NOT NULL default CURRENT_TIMESTAMP,
`action` varchar(20)  NOT NULL,
`page` varchar(255)  NOT NULL,
`referer` varchar(255)  NOT NULL,
`browser` varchar(200)  NOT NULL,
`timeSpent` int(6) unsigned NOT NULL,
`vars` text  NOT NULL,
PRIMARY KEY  (`id`)
) ;
```

2. Open up `prepend.inc.php`. We will write a function to collect tracking information and insert it into the `trackingData` table.

3. Add the following `logUserTrail()` function in `prepend.inc.php`—add it after the `debug()` function definition. In the function, we insert the current request URI, all the variables associated with it, the last page, etc. into the table. We also save the ID of the tracking data item into the session. In the next call to this function, when we find the `tdId`, we update that record with the time spent on that page—which will be the current time minus `accessTime` for that request.

```php
function logUserTrail()
{
    $userId = isset($_SESSION['userId']) ? $_SESSION['userId'] : 0;
    $page = "http://".getenv('HTTP_HOST').getenv('REQUEST_URI');
    // If trackingId of last request is set, update its timeSpent
    if (isset($_SESSION['tdId']))
    {
        $query = "UPDATE trackingData SET timeSpent =
            NOW() - accessTime WHERE id = '".$_SESSION['tdId']."'";
        $GLOBALS['db']->Query($query);
    }
// Insert current request information in trackingData
$query = "INSERT INTO trackingData (userId, sessionId, action,
                                    page, referer, browser, vars)
VALUES ($userId, '".$_REQUEST["PHPSESSID"]."', '".$_
                                REQUEST['action']."', '$page',
 '".getenv('HTTP_REFERER')."', '".getenv(
            'HTTP_USER_AGENT')."', '".serialize($_REQUEST)."')";
$GLOBALS['db']->Query($query);
$_SESSION['tdId'] = $GLOBALS['db']->GetCurrentId();
}
```

4. Now open `index.php` and call the function we just wrote. We should do it before including the action file.

```
$action = isset($_REQUEST["action"]) ? $_REQUEST["action"] : "home";
$file = $action . ".inc.php";
logUserTrail();
if (in_array($action, $validActions) && is_file($file) )
{
    include($file);
}
```

5. Now access the POTR site. Browse around on a few pages. Confirm that the data is inserting into the table through your favorite administration tool.

6. Our tracking mechanism is now in place. After a few requests, doing a query like `SELECT userId, action, timeSpent, browser, vars from trackingData` may give an output similar to what is shown in the next screenshot. Notice the vars field gives us values that tell us the exact action the user was trying to perform. In the highlighted case, a non logged in user was on the first step of the order process, and spent 4 seconds on it.

userId	action	timeSpent	browser	vars
0		7	OPWV-SDK UP.Browser/7.0.2.3.119 (GUI) MMP/2.0 Push...	a:0:{}
0	order	4	OPWV-SDK UP.Browser/7.0.2.3.119 (GUI) MMP/2.0 Push...	a:4:{s:6:"action";s:5:"order";s:4:"step";s:1:"1";s...
0	order	1	OPWV-SDK UP.Browser/7.0.2.3.119 (GUI) MMP/2.0 Push...	a:8: {s:9:"PHPSESSID";s:32:"46a448d178f69f5134a7e30...
0	order	1	OPWV-SDK UP.Browser/7.0.2.3.119 (GUI) MMP/2.0 Push...	a:8: {s:9:"PHPSESSID";s:32:"46a448d178f69f5134a7e30...
0	order	2	OPWV-SDK UP.Browser/7.0.2.3.119 (GUI) MMP/2.0 Push...	a:7: {s:9:"PHPSESSID";s:32:"46a448d178f69f5134a7e30...
0	order	9	OPWV-SDK UP.Browser/7.0.2.3.119 (GUI) MMP/2.0 Push...	a:12: {s:9:"PHPSESSID";s:32:"46a448d178f69f5134a7e3...
0		9	Nokia6600/1.0 (3.49.1) SymbianOS/7.0s Series60/2.0...	a:0:{}
0		9	SonyEricssonK750i/R1L Browser/SEMC-Browser/4.2 Pro...	a:0:{}

How is All the Data Tracked?

The `logUserTrail()` function gets called on every request to our site. In the function, we can get the current page and last page links using the `HTTP_REQUEST_URI` and `HTTP_REFERER` server-side variables. We are storing the session and user IDs so that we can run queries on them later. The `serialize()` function takes all the variables in the current request and converts them into a string. This will allow us to track the actual step in the order process or the address the user was entering.

We can now query the collected data and get insights into how customers are using our application. Some interesting queries could be:

- Find all exit pages: `SELECT * FROM trackingData WHERE timeSpent = 0`
- Find pages slow to process for the user: `SELECT * FROM trackingData WHERE timeSpent > 20`.
- Find popular modules: `SELECT action, count(*) as total FROM trackingData GROUP BY action ORDER BY total DESC`.

Covering Problem Areas

We are just tracking successful requests in the current process. If we add an HTTP error handler page, we can also track causes of HTTP errors like 404, 500 or others. We can also add an exception/error handler in PHP, which can track the source of problems in PHP code as well. This data can be linked to the session/user ID and we can have a complete picture of what was happening when the error occurred.

Tapping into the Device Data

We are tracking the user's browser. We can link it up with the WURFL data we have and generate insights into which devices are used most, what are their capabilities, and how can we exploit them.

Making it Easier to Ask for Help

Despite all this, if the user faces a problem, we want to make it easier to ask for support. This can be done simply by creating a feedback page, and linking it up from the footer navigation. The form will allow the user to add comments, will include the tracking `data ID`, and send us an email with full details.

We are not including code for this here! You can build it on your own, or check it out in the source code you may download from the book website.

Luigi, our dear client, is very excited with all this. We mentioned that he wants to add many interactive features to POTR now. But before that, let's see what we did in this chapter.

Summary

In this chapter, we focussed on what we should do to ensure that our mobile site is delivered well to most customers. Specifically:

- We tested POTR with ready.mobi. We saw the different tests it carries out and notes it shows. It's not necessary to fix all problems, but it helps!

- We also saw the different recommendations and best practices about mobile web development. We referenced W3C's Mobile Web Best Practices, Luca Passani's Global Authoring Practices, and built a checklist we can use on our projects.

- Following recommendations may not be enough. We started tracking user data on POTR through our central `index.php` file.

In the next chapter, we will look at how we can push updates to customers via SMS. Luigi has been pushing for this feature for quite some time, and we are now ready to take it up!

6
Sending Text Messages

SMS-based applications have taken the mobile world by a storm. According to research, there are two types of mobile users: texters and talkers. It was observed that the texters send more than double the messages that talkers do. SMS for them is a non-obtrusive way of communication.

In this chapter, we will learn about sending text messages, and in the process learn the fundamentals of using third-party services for messaging.

We will specifically take look at:

- Updating order status for POTR
- Selecting an SMS gateway provider and setting up an account
- Sending text messages using the gateway's API
- Understanding how SMS is delivered
- Getting delivery status updates
- Setting up our own SMS gateway
- Sending bulk messages

We have almost completed the XHTML MP part of POTR and Luigi wants to build more interaction into the system now. He wants to send order updates to the customers via SMS. After we did a bit of research, we found that the job is easier than we think. Let's take a look.

Updating Order Status

Once Luigi's got the order, he will prepare the pizzas and dispatch them. He wants to update the order status in the system, so that his task of tracking orders becomes easier. He also wants to send out an SMS notification to the customers telling them that their order will reach them within half an hour. Before we can send out the SMS, we need to build an order update process. Let's see how the task becomes straightforward with our existing framework.

Time for Action: Updating Order Status

1. We kept a provision for different order statuses when we designed the orders table. The status field is an enumerated field, and can contain one of the three values: N for New order, P for orders in Process, and C for Completed orders. Let's add a function to our Order class to update this field. The following code shows the function:

```php
public function UpdateStatus($status)
{
    $query = "UPDATE ".$this->table." SET status = '$status'
            WHERE id = '".$this->_id."'";
    if ($GLOBALS["db"]->UpdateQuery($query))
    {
        $this->status = $status;
        return true;
    }
    return false;
}
```

2. Next, let's list new orders. For this, we query the orders table for all orders with status "N". With each item in the list, we will add a checkbox so that we can mark them as dispatched. Let us make a new file processOrders. inc.php for this. We also need to add the action "processOrders" to the $validActions array in index.php. The following code shows the code to generate this list:

```php
<?php
// File to process orders and mark them as dispatched
$prodObj = new Product();
$products = $prodObj->GetAll("categoryId = 1", "priority asc");
$varObj = new Variation();
$varObj = $varObj->GetAll("", "type asc");
$ordObj = new Order($prodObj, $varObj);

// Load all new orders
$pendingOrders = $ordObj->GetAll("status = 'N'", "orderDate asc");
echo '<h2>Process New Orders</h2>';
if (count($pendingOrders) > 0)
{
    echo '<form action="index.php" method="POST">
    <fieldset>
    <input type="hidden" name="action" value=
                                "processOrders" /><ul>';
    foreach($pendingOrders as $order)
    {
        $date = date("m/d/y h:i", strtotime($order['orderDate']));
```

```
echo '<li><input type="checkbox" name="orderIds[]"
checked="checked" value="'.$order['id'].'"/>
<b>'.$order['id'].' ('.$date.') $'.$order['total'].'</b> <br
/>'.$order['address1'].' '.$order['address2'].',
'.$order['city'].' <i>'.$order['phone'].'</i></li>';
    }
    echo '</ul><input type="submit" class="button"
                            name="option" value="Update Orders" />
    </fieldset></form>';
}
else
{
    echo '<p>No pending orders to process. <a href="?action=
                            processOrders">Check again.</a></p>';
}
?>
```

3. When we run the code, it will show up as in the following screenshot.

4. Once the form is submitted, we will get the selected orders' IDs in the `$orderIds` array. We can loop over this, and call the UpdateStatus method to change the status in the table. We add the following code right after creating `$orderObj` in `processOrders.inc.php`.

```
// If we got order IDs to process, do that
if ($_REQUEST['orderIds'])
{
    echo "<h2>Processing...</h2>";
    $updated = 0;
    foreach($_REQUEST['orderIds'] as $orderId)
    {
        $ordObj->Load($orderId);
        // Change the status to 'Processing...'
        if ($ordObj->UpdateStatus('P'))
        {
            $updated++;
        }
    }
    echo "<p>$updated orders updated.</p>";
}
```

5. When processed, the page will update the selected orders, and show any new orders. Luigi can keep refreshing the page and dispatching the orders. If there are no orders to process, the page will show "No pending orders".

Now that we have order status updates taken care of, let's get to the core of the Luigi's requirement—sending order dispatch notification to customers via SMS.

Sending SMS Notifications

There are two approaches to sending SMS from a server. You can either connect a phone/modem to the server and set up your own system or use a third party SMS gateway service.

We will look at sending messages from your own server later in the chapter. For now, we will focus on SMS gateways. SMS gateways provide an API or web service that you can call to send messages.

Getting Started with a Gateway

We will use Clickatell (www.clickatell.com) as our SMS gateway service provider. Clickatell can send messages to almost all mobile networks in the world at competitive rates. It also offers a variety of methods to use its API. HTTP is the most common, in which you send GET or POST requests to its API to send messages.

Time for Action: Registering on Clickatell

1. Go to www.clickatell.com, and register for an account with it.

2. In the registration process, Clickatell will send you the confirmation codes via email and SMS. Enter them in to confirm your registration.

3. Now go to www.clickatell.com again and login to Clickatell Central using your login details.

4. Because Clickatell offers multiple connection types, you need to create a link first. Go to **My Connections** from the menu and select to add an **HTTP** connection. The following screenshot shows the kind of form you will see.

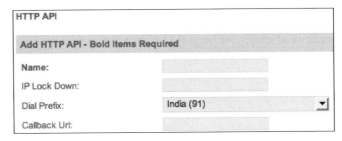

5. At the minimum, you need to enter a name for this connection. You can also enter the IP range that can invoke this connection, the default country to send messages to (so that a zero at the start of the phone number will be replaced with that country code), and also a URL where status updates can be sent.

6. After submitting the form, you have the new connection set up. Each connection has an API ID that you need to pass to the gateway while establishing a connection. The API ID is the most important piece of information in a connection. The next screenshot shows summary info about our newly created POTR connection. We are now ready to use Clickatell!

Name	Type	API ID	Dialing Code	Last Used
potr	HTTP	3015229	91	Unknown

Connection Types

Different gateways offer different connection types. They may offer any of the following methods:

- HTTP/HTTPS: Sending data through GET or POST submission to a URL.
- SMTP: Sending a message using email, either from a desktop client or a server.
- FTP: Typically, for bulk messaging. Upload a text file to an FTP server with request parameters.
- XML: Send XML data over HTTP to the API. This makes it easier to send messages in a batch.
- SMPP: Binary socket connection with the gateway. Typically, used for higher-end applications.
- COM Object: Not very common, but allows connection using a COM object from Windows applications.

Integrating with Clickatell

We are selecting the HTTP method to integrate with Clickatell. HTTP is familiar to web developers, easy to use, and offers many features. You can pass parameters to the API as variables in a GET or POST request. Apart from that, HTTP is also supported by most gateways. A request to send an SMS looks like the following on Clickatell:

```
http://api.clickatell.com/http/sendmsg?api_id=xxxx&user=xxxx&password
=xxxx&to=xxxx&text=xxxx
```

You can send a test message by entering the URL in your browser and replacing xxxx with proper values. Keep in mind that every message costs! Most gateways will provide some free credits or discounted rates for test messages, but the meter keeps running for every message you send! Our meter for Luigi is also running, so let us proceed with integrating the Clickatell API into the POTR code.

We will first write a wrapper class to integrate with Clickatell. This will keep the integration distinct from other code, and make it easier to manage changes. Essentially, it will send GET requests and process the response. Here is how the API works for Clickatell:

To Authenticate and Get a Session:

- Command: `http://api.clickatell.com/http/auth?api_id=xxxx&user=xxxx&password=xxxx`.
- Response: `OK: Session ID` or `ERR: Error number`.

To Send an SMS after Authenticating:

- Command: `http://api.clickatell.com/http/sendmsg?session_id=xxxx&to=xxxx&text=xxxx`.
- Response: `ID: apimsgid` or `ERR: Error number`

Based on this, let's write up our wrapper class.

Time for Action: Integrating with Clickatell to Send SMS Notifications

1. The first step in Clickatell integration is to authenticate and get a session ID. We can use this session ID in all further requests. Let us start our `SMSGateway` class with some basic variables and initialization functions.

```php
<?php
class SMSGateway
{
    private $apiURL;
    private $apiId;
    private $sessionId;
    public $lastCommand;
    public $lastResult;
    public function __construct()
    {
        $this->apiURL = "http://api.clickatell.com/http/";
    }
```

```
public function Init($username, $password, $apiId)
{
    $this->apiId = $apiId;
    $params['user'] = $username;
    $params['password'] = $password;
    $params['api_id'] = $this->apiId;
    $command = 'auth';
    if ($this->Request($command, $params))
    {
        return true;
    }
}
}
?>
```

2. The request function takes the name of the command and an array of parameters to pass. We will make a HTTP GET request to the Clickatell API URL and process the response string. The basic pattern of the response string is two parts separated by a colon. The first part is the status code and the second part is the value. So for authentication, we will get "OK: Session ID". If there is an error, we will get "ERR: Error number". Let us write the function now. The following code shows the implementation.

```
public function Request($command, $params)
{
    $url = $this->apiURL.$command.'?';
    // Add the session ID to requests
    if ($command != "auth" && $this->sessionId != "")
    {
        $params['session_id'] = $this->sessionId;
    }
    foreach($params as $key=>$value)
    {
        $url .= "&$key=".urlencode($value);
    }
    try
    {
        // PHP's file() function can make HTTP GET requests and
        //                                      return the response
        // So let's just use that for now
        $response = file($url);
        $resultArr = explode(":", $response[0]);
        $this->lastResult = trim($resultArr[1]);
        if ($resultArr[0] == "ERR")
        {
```

```
                    $this->lastResult = "ERR";
                    return false;
                }
                else
                {
                    switch($command)
                    {
                        case "auth":
                            $this->sessionId = $this->lastResult;
                            break;
                        default:
                            break;
                    }
                    return true;
                }
            }
            catch (Exception $ex)
            {
                // Problem, could not process the request
                $this->lastResult = "ERR";
                return false;
            }
        }
```

3. Now that the basics are in place, let us write a function to make a "Send" request. We need the number to send the message to, the "from" number, and the actual message. We can even validate the phone number using some pattern. But for now, let's perform basic cleanups of removing spaces and the '+' sign from the number. The following code shows the Send and CleanUpPhoneNumber functions.

```
public function CleanUpPhoneNumber($phone)
{
    $phone = trim($phone);
    $phone = str_replace(" ", "", $phone);
    $phone = str_replace("+", "", $phone);
    return $phone;
}
public function Send($to, $from, $msg)
{
    $command = "sendmsg";
    $to = $this->CleanUpPhoneNumber($to);
    if ($to == "")
    {
        return 0;
```

```
    }
    $params['to'] = $to;
    $params['from'] = $from;
    $params['text'] = $msg;
    $message = new Message();
    if ($this->Request($command, $params))
    {
        return $this->lastResult;
    }
    return 0;
}
```

4. The important parts here are the "sendmsg" command, and to, from, and text parameters. They tell Clickatell to queue the message for delivery.

5. Let us modify our `processOrders.inc.php` and add SMS sending to it. When the status is changed from new to processing, we will send a message to the customer, notifying her or him that the pizzas are on their way! To do this, initialize an `SMSGateway` object, authenticate with the gateway, and then send out messages in a loop. The following code highlights the modifications to the `processOrders.inc.php` code for this.

```
// If we got order IDs to process, do that
if ($_REQUEST['orderIds'])
{
    echo "<h2>Processing...</h2>";
    // First, authenticate with the SMS Gateway
    $sms = new SMSGateway();
    // Pass Clickatell username, password and API ID
    if (!$sms->Init("username", "password", "3015229"))
    {
        $msg =  "Could not authenticate with SMS Gateway.";
    }
    $updated = 0;
    $sent = 0;
    foreach($_REQUEST['orderIds'] as $orderId)
    {
        $ordObj->Load($orderId);
        // Change the status to 'Processing...'
        if ($ordObj->UpdateStatus('P'))
        {
            $updated++;
        }
        $msg = "Order dispatched. Pizzas will reach you within
                                    30 minutes. - POTR";
        // Now send an SMS: to, from, message
```

```
        if ($sms->Send($ordObj->phone, "170212345678", $msg))
        {
            $sent++;
        }
    }
    echo "<p>$updated orders updated. <b>$sent messages sent.<
                                                    /b></p>";
}
```

6. Congratulations! This completes sending SMS notifications when orders are dispatched. The screen for Luigi will look similar to the following screenshot.

Processing...

1 orders updated. **1 messages sent.**

Process New Orders

No pending orders to process. Check again.

7. Well, we should fix the grammar on that page to take care of singulars, but we expect a lot of orders! So let's keep it at that for now, and see what happened here.

What Just Happened?

Our SMSGateway class creates a URL to call based on the command and the parameters. The first command is to authenticate, so it does that in the Init() function. The Request() function makes the actual request via the file() function. At this time, the Clickatell gateway receives the requests, confirms the validity of the session or login information, and sends back a result.

The result is in two parts separated by a colon. The first part is the status code and the second the actual value. Our Request() function splits the response at the colon, and checks if the status code is an error. If it is, we return false. We also store the latest result from Clickatell in the lastResult variable in all cases. This can be used later, e.g., to store the session ID so that we can pass it with subsequent requests.

We have hard-coded the API ID and From number in our code. Ideally, it should come from a configuration file. The rest of the code is to update the table and show the result to the administrator.

This is what happens on our server. But how does the message actually reach the customer? Let's see how.

So What Happens at the Gateway?

Clickatell, or any other SMS gateway, is connected to multiple mobile operator networks. Using the SMSC (Short Message Service Center) of the operator, they send out messages. Take a look at the following figure; it explains how a message is sent from our website to the mobile device.

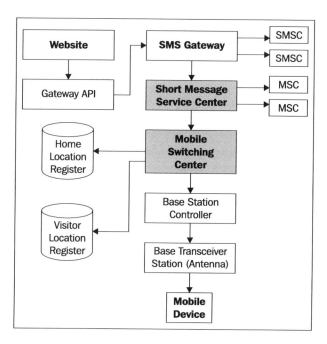

SMSC (Short Message Service Center) and MSC (Mobile Switching Center) are the most important parts of the process. SMSC is a store and forward agent; it stores the messages to be sent and tries to deliver them via an appropriate switching center. Consider that the job of an MSC is very much like that of a network switch—routing information as necessary. The SMS Service Center now checks with the Home Location Register (HLR) and Visitor Location Register (VLR) to see where the mobile device is. If you are roaming outside your home location, you will be registered in the Visitor Location Register in that particular location. When you come back to the home location, you will be registered in the Home Location Register. The registers essentially keep a track of your presence! Once it is confirmed where the device is and that it is available, the message is sent to the MSC, and MSC delivers it to the mobile through the Base Station Controller (BSC) and Base Transceiver Station (BTS). The job of BSC and BTS is to interact with the device via the cellular network. If the mobile is out of range, the destination MSC will notify the SMSC when it comes back in range; and the SMSC will resend the message. The SMSC typically stores the message for one day, but the validity period can be set by the sender as well.

Because SMS gateways are connected to many mobile networks, they intelligently select the route to send the message through. SMSCs can also provide acknowledgement of the message delivery and the gateway may pass it back to the website.

If your head is not spinning with all the jargon, let's look at some more. If it is, chill, it's only the jargon that's difficult. The fundamentals are easy to understand! Check out the "Mobile Messaging Jargon File" box for some easier, more frequently used terms!

Mobile Messaging Jargon File

Flash Message: Short message that is displayed immediately on receipt on the mobile device's screen.

Mobile Originated (MO): A message sent (originating) from a mobile device to an application or another device.

Mobile Terminated (MT): A message sent from an application to (terminating on) a mobile device.

Shortcode: A short (usually 4 digits) number that is used in premium SMS services to send messages to. Generally, the same shortcode is available across multiple mobile operators.

Finding Message Delivery Status

We are sending out messages, but don't have a way to find out if they get delivered. Unless we find that out, we are not really sure what happens to them. We won't even know how much time it takes to deliver messages! Luigi can't live in a limbo like this, so let us build a mechanism to track messages.

Time for Action: Tracking Queued Messages

1. Create a table called "messages". The fields will be id (primary key), gwId (gateway message ID), requestDate, to (phone number), message (the actual message), and status (enum: Q for queued, G for delivered to upstream gateway, R for received, and F for failed).

2. Create a class "Message" extending the BaseModel. Add variables to map to the table fields. This is simply a data holder class and will look like the following code.

```
class Message extends BaseModel
{
    public $_to;
    public $_message;
    public $_requestDate;
```

```
public $_status;
public $_gwId;
public function __construct($tableName = "messages",
                                          $data = null)
{
    parent::__construct($tableName, $data);
}
}
```

3. We can now instantiate the `message` class when we are sending the SMS in the `SMSGateway` class. Populate the values in it and save it to the table. The `Save()` function will give us the auto-incremented primary key of the table, and that in turn can be passed to the Clickatell gateway as client message ID. The following code shows the modified `Send()` method in the `SMSGateway` class.

```
public function Send($to, $from, $msg)
{
    $command = "sendmsg";
    $to = $this->CleanUpPhoneNumber($to);
    if ($to == "")
    {
        return 0;
    }
    $params['to'] = $to;
    $params['from'] = $from;
    $params['text'] = $msg;
    $message = new Message();
    $message->to = $to;
    $message->message = $msg;
    $message->requestDate = date("Y-m-d H:i:s");
    if ($message->Save())
    {
        $params['climsgid'] = $message->id;
        if ($this->Request($command, $params))
        {
            $message->gwId = $this->lastResult;
            $message->status = 'Q';
            if ($message->Save())
            {
                return $this->lastResult;
            }
        }
    }
    return 0;
}
```

4. We now have records being inserted every time a message is queued onto Clickatell!

Querying for Message Status

If you noticed, the messages are saved with default blank status first. Once we get the result from the gateway, we update the message row with "Q" as the status. This way if a message's status is blank, it means it was never queued to the gateway.

Clickatell returns an ID for each message we queue—which is what we store in the `gwId` field. We can use that ID to check the status of the message delivery. The Clickatell API to check message status is like the following:

- Command: `http://api.clickatell.com/http/querymsg?session_id=xxx&apimsgid=XXXXX`.

- Response: `ID: xxxx Status: xxxx` or `ERR: Error number`.

We can even use the client message ID (`climsgid`) to query message status. Integrating the `querymsg` command with our class is simple. We can add a new function `QueryStatus($gwId)` and make a request to the gateway. Clickatell returns numeric codes for the status (refer to the Clickatell API documentation at `http://support.clickatell.com`). We can process the returned status code and update our message table accordingly.

What we are doing here is polling for message status. Polling is a good solution when you want the status of particular messages, but Clickatell provides another method for getting message status. And this method pushes status updates to us, rather than our pulling them!

Lessen the Load with Status Update Callbacks

While we set up the connection type on Clickatell, we can also specify a callback URL. If set, the gateway will make a GET request to that URL every time the status of a queued message changes. This reduces the load on both your server and Clickatell, as there is no polling required. Clickatell returns `apiMsgId`, `cliMsgId`, `api_id`, `to`, `timestamp`, `from`, `status`, and `charge` values to the callback. The URL must be publicly accessible so that Clickatell can call it, which means it may not work in your test environment.

Apart from setting up the callback URL in preferences for the connection, you also need to pass `"deliv_ack"` and `"callback"` parameters in the `"sendmsg"` command. Queuing the message now will keep updating you when it is accepted by the gateway, forwarded to an upstream gateway in the mobile network, and received on the device. We are not covering the details of callback implementation here because they are well documented and Clickatell specific.

Callbacks are an important feature of a gateway. There are other gateways that provide similar features and you can check with the gateway you choose about callbacks beforehand. Actually, there are many things you should check before selecting your SMS gateway. Let's review what you should check!

Before You Decide on a Gateway

We used Clickatell for POTR. But you can select any SMS gateway that you like. There are many service providers in this area and finding the right gateway can be confusing. For starters, you can review the list on Developers' Home: `http://www.developershome.com/sms/smsGatewayProvComp.asp` or the listing on Dmoz: `http://dmoz.org/Computers/Mobile_Computing/Wireless_Data/Short_Messaging_Service/`. After that, you can Google for SMS gateways in your region. You will get many results. If you have many choices, you need some guidelines on selecting the best one.

Here are a few things you can keep in mind while deciding on the gateway:

- The idea is to find the cheapest, most reliable, and easiest SMS gateway! There is no single choice for all these requirements. So the starting step is to clearly know what you want!

- SMS sending charges can be either credit-based or per message. One credit need not always mean one message. Gateways that show better messages/ credit ratio may have higher price for each credit.

- Identify the countries you want to send messages to. Not all gateways serve all countries.

- Check the reliability of the network. If you can, send a test message from the gateway to determine the delay in delivery.

- How many messages will you be sending? There are volume discounts.

- Charges also vary according to the destination country and mobile network. How many will you be sending where?

- Check out hidden costs. Set up costs or taxes may be hidden.

- Some gateways will also have minimum purchase commitments. Factor this in when you do your estimates.

- Check the validity of the package you buy. You don't want it to expire unused!

- What are the different ways to connect to the gateway? Most support HTTP access. If you require SMPP, XML or any other, check right at the start.

- You should also check the level and type of support available. Are the APIs well documented? Can you find enough examples on the provider's site as well as on other sources? (Try Googling a bit!)

- Check the type of reports and stats you will have. Your credits can disappear very quickly, and you want to be on top of it! A gateway that can provide you alerts when the credit level falls below a threshold is great!

- Does the gateway provide a callback service? How will you know the delivery status of the message?

- How can you send bulk SMS? Is there an easy way for it?

- Do you want to send MMS/WAP Push or other type of messages? If so, will the gateway support it?

- If you require two-way messaging, check now! Lot of gateways do not provide this service.

- Similarly, if you want short codes, check the availability and costs associated with them. Typically, there will be a setup fee and minimum commitment with shortcodes as well.

- You can even use multiple SMS gateways. Depending on the feature required or the network, you can queue your messages on any of them.

Sending SMS from Your Own Computer

We promised we will tell you more about sending SMS from your own computer/server earlier! Now is the time for that!

You can connect a phone or GSM/GPRS/CDMA modem to your computer and send out messages. GSM/CDMA modems come in various types. External modems that connect to the computer via serial interface and take a SIM card are most popular. Most mobile phones come with some kind of PC communication suite software these days. Such software will allow you to send out messages from the computer. If you want to send messages from another application, you will need to use a software that exposes message-sending APIs—either through a socket connection or via command line. Here are some resources that will help you in setting up your own gateway:

- Kannel (`www.kannel.org`) is the most popular WAP/SMS gateway in the open-source world.

- Gnokii (`www.gnokii.org`) can also connect to a phone and send/receive messages.

- PlaySMS (`http://playsms.sourceforge.net`) is a set of PHP scripts that can integrate with Kannel, Gnokii, Uplink, and Clickatell.

- SMS Link (`http://smslink.sourceforge.net`) is another SMS server using a serially attached GSM device.

- Developers' Home has some other free SMS libraries listed as well: `http://www.developershome.com/sms/freeLibForSMS.asp`.

There are many commercial SMS gateway software solutions that can connect to a phone or special GSM modem. Search online for "SMS Gateway" and you will get a long list!

Setting up your own SMS gateway may not be simple. You would opt for this option if you want maximum control and have reliable hardware to send out messages. It's better to use third-party gateways otherwise.

Sending Bulk Messages

Broadcasting messages to a wide audience is a common requirement. Luigi might want to inform all his customers about a special offer for this evening via SMS. We can do this by looping over our customer list and sending out messages. But that would involve too many connections to the gateway—which will be slow.

There are easier methods for this purpose. Clickatell, and many other gateways, allow sending comma-separated multiple phone numbers in the "to" parameter. You may start a batch of messages and do a mail merge type operation. With some gateways, you can send phone numbers via text file or XML.

If your requirements are bigger, consider using SMPP (Short Message Peer-to-Peer Protocol) for connecting to the gateway. SMPP provides reliable and fast communication with the gateway. There is a bit of learning curve with SMPP-based integration, but it will pay off for large projects.

For us, we are happy with our current messaging setup. It's time to take a quick look at what we learned!

Summary

In this chapter, we learned to send SMS messages to our customers. Specifically:

- We built a system to update order status for POTR.
- We learned how to set-up an account with Clickatell and how the gateway APIs work. We then created the SMSGateway wrapper class.
- We then saw how an SMS is delivered from the website to the mobile device, through SMSC and MSC.
- We touched upon using callbacks for message status updates.
- We learned how to query the message status and send bulk messages.
- We also got an overview of setting up our own SMS gateway and guidelines for selecting a third-party gateway.

Luigi has a new idea of sending special offers with photographs via MMS now. In the next chapter, we will look at how we can do just that!

7
Adding Spice to Messages: MMS

Sending text messages to customers allowed us to instantly connect with our customers. Our SMS work has been very rewarding for Luigi and Pizza On the Run. This small update removed the customers' anxiety! Luigi has now started sending special offers via SMS.

Excited as he is, Luigi now wants to explore Multimedia Messaging Service (MMS) and send out special offers with a photo of the dish. He even has a new idea to engage customers in a community by asking them to share their pizza party photos and testimonials. It would be fun to see everyone eating our pizzas and posing for the camera! Let's figure it out then!

In this chapter, we will work on:

- Creating Multimedia Messages for special offers at POTR
- Controlling message presentation
- Sending Multimedia Messages through our gateway
- Receiving photos from customers via MMS

MMS is a popular means to circulate porn videos and movie trailers, but there is certainly a lot more to it than that! Let's create an MMS message and understand more about it.

Creating a "Special Offers" MMS message

We want to send a message with a 'special offer' and a pizza image. There are many ways to send such an MMS message. We can:

- Compose it using a mobile device and send it from there.
- Compose using a mobile device, send it as an email, and send it to customers from there.
- Write a script to generate an MMS message through an MMS library or SDK. Send out via an MMS gateway.
- Compose using Nokia, Openwave (or any other) toolkit and send it via the server.

We are interested in the last two options. Let us look at how to compose and preview an MMS message using Nokia tools.

Time for Action: Compose an MMS message using Nokia Tools

1. We will use the "Nokia Mobile Internet Toolkit" (NMIT) and "Series 60 Content Authoring SDK 2.0 for Symbian OS" (SDK). Download and register them from http://forum.nokia.com/tools/. You will also need to get a serial key for NMIT. The tools and accompanying documentation are completely free though. Make sure you have both of them installed.

2. Open NMIT, go to **File** menu, and select **New**. You will see a screen similar to the one shown in the following screenshot. Go to the **Messaging** tab and select **MMS Wizard**.

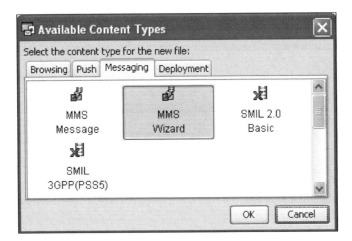

3. The first thing we need to tell the wizard is whether we are trying to send a message or receive one. We will be sending the message, so select **m-send-req**.

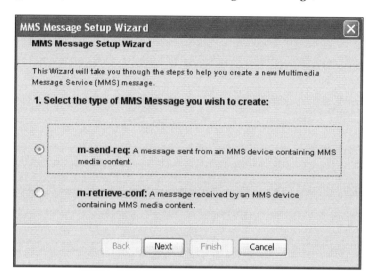

4. The next screen will ask for recipient address. MMS messages can be sent to email addresses, mobile devices, or IP addresses. The wizard shows you examples of the three types of addresses you can enter. For now, we enter an email address. Notice the < and > around the email address. Some MMS gateways will not be able to send the email if you skip them. On the same screen, you can also enter the subject of the MMS message and any address to which you want to CC the message.

5. We are now at a stage to create the actual content of the message. Create a text file with the special offer message, and pick up an image you wish to send. We are using the POTR logo and `special_offer.txt`. The following screenshot shows the picked files. Minimum supported formats are text, images (JPG, GIF, WBMP, 160x120 pixels), audio (AMR), and calendar (vCard, vCalendar). The newer devices also support MP3 audio and MP4/3GP video.

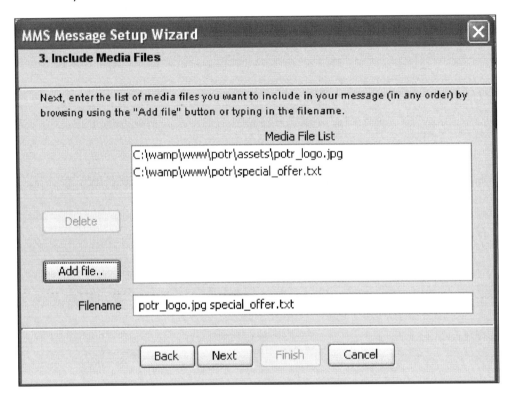

6. Step 4 of the wizard asks whether you have an SMIL file or you would like it to auto-generate it. SMIL (pronounced "smile") files are used to control the presentation of our message. For now, let the system auto-generate the file. Later in the chapter, we will see how we can customize the file.

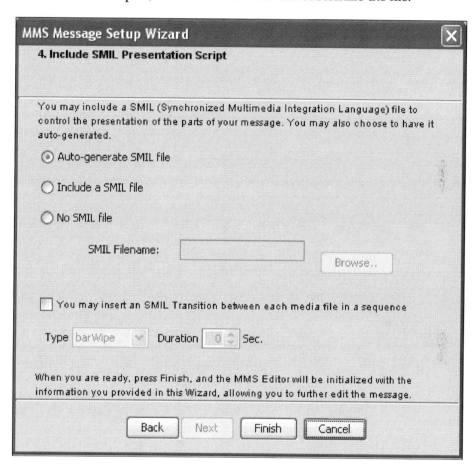

7. You should now see a screen like the one shown in the following screenshot. The top part shows message headers that will be sent out. You can specify an ID for the message, date, to, and from among other things. The bottom half of the screen is the MMS content. The bottom left shows you the files you added. The bottom right shows how the files will be encoded for the message and properties you can set for encoding. MMS messages are binary messages and need to be encoded in a particular way.

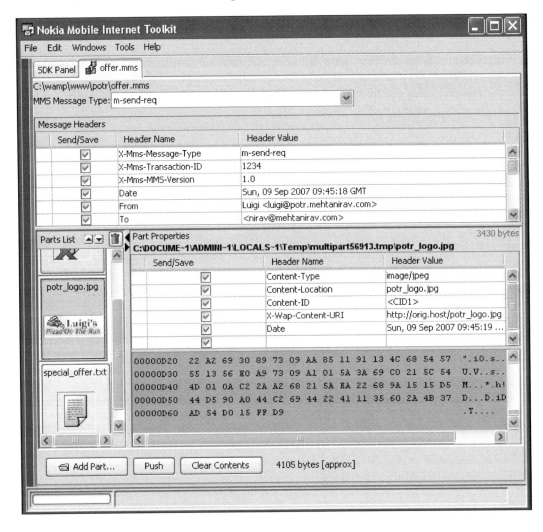

8. We have our first MMS message ready now. Save it on disk so that we can edit it later. We now want to preview how it will look on a mobile device.

9. Go to the SDK panel in NMIT. The Content Authoring SDK will show up on the right-hand side. Click the green button next to the SDK name to start an instance of it. This will launch the Series 60 emulator.

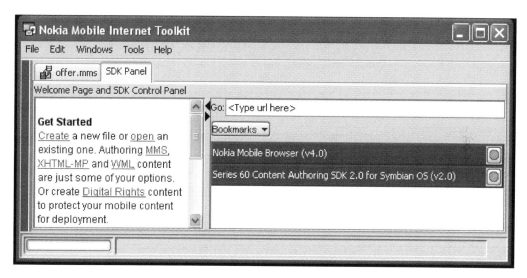

10. After the SDK has started, come back to the MMS tab and click on the **Push** button at the bottom. This will send the message to the SDK.

11. Go to the Message Inbox on the SDK emulator and our MMS message message should be there. Open it and you can view the message. The following screenshot shows how this will look like on the SDK.

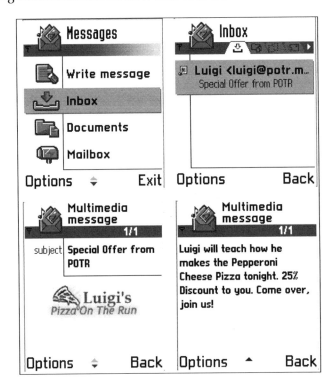

What Just Happened: Understanding MMS Structure

As we added different files, the Nokia toolkit encoded them in a particular way. When we clicked push, it placed the MMS message in the emulator's Inbox. Just like normal email and SMS, MMS messages could be plain-text. Or like an email with attachments, they could contain multiple parts. Such messages are called multipart—one message contains multiple files—each in its own part, separated by a boundary. If you want to understand the structure of MMS, you need to understand these three different types of multipart messages:

- Multipart-related: Apart from the content parts, there is also a special presentation part at the beginning of the message. This part refers to other parts and determines how the message will be displayed. We created a multipart-related message in the example.

- Multipart-alternative: Some devices supported alternative presentation files—SMIL or XHTML for example. When you include both XHTML and SMIL for presentation, if the device supports XHTML in MMS, it will use that. On other devices, SMIL will be used. The order of including these files is in order of complexity. Simplest first. So first SMIL and then XHTML.

- Multipart-mixed: If you just want your files shown sequentially or treated like attachments, you can use multipart-mixed.

The following screenshot shows how a multipart-alternative message may be constructed. Each part inside the body has a Content ID or Content Location that is used to refer to that file in the presentation.

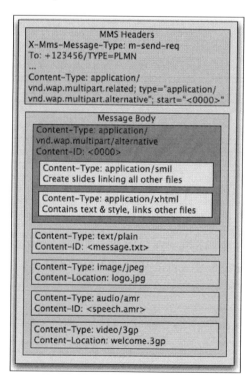

The message type, recipient addresses, and subject that we entered in the example above go in the MMS headers. If you noticed, you could enter your own headers or modify some default values for headers in the NMIT MMS composer. One header you may like to know about is "X-Mms-Message-Class". This header determines the type of message, and the value could be Personal, Advertisement, Informational, or Auto. Use an appropriate value for your messages.

The SMIL file that NMIT automatically generated is an XML file that defines how the logo and special offer text would be placed. We will look at SMIL in a bit more detail later in the chapter.

When you clicked the **Push** button, NMIT encoded all the content together in a binary format and sent it to the Content Authoring SDK. Unlike emails, you can't see the body of an MMS message with a text editor. There are set standards about how the headers should be constructed and how different elements should be referenced. If we use a Hex Editor to open the file, it would look like the following screenshot. The SDK decodes this format and shows it up as an MMS message. If you wanted to write your own MMS decoder, you would need to understand this format!

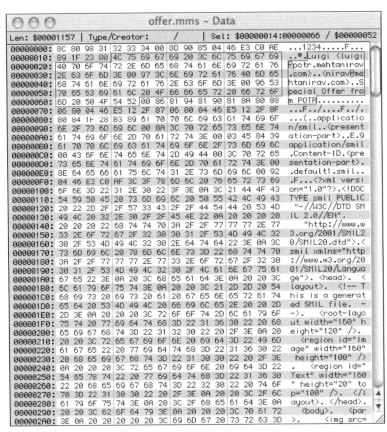

Want to Know More about MMS?

MMS is a vast subject. There are different things that happen to MMS—from construction to read receipts. A search on Google may not always take you to the best information on the topic. Openwave and Nokia Forum have very good material on MMS and developing MMS applications. You should read the articles and documentation available at both these places before you look at the MMS specs from `www.3gpp.org` or `www.openmobilealliance.org`. Openwave and Nokia also have tools that you can use to encode and decode MMS using a programming language. Later in the chapter, we will look at MMSDecoder—a PHP library to process MMS.

Hold on before you create too many special offers!

Creating and sending MMS messages is not very difficult. But sending too many messages can get you in trouble. Sending unsolicited SMS/MMS messages is considered as spam and many countries have strict laws against it. Even if you are collecting customer phone numbers on your site, make sure you have an appropriate "Privacy Policy" and "Terms of Use" to safeguard you. At the same time, make subscription completely opt-in and allow for an easy unsubscribe procedure. We don't want to irritate our customers; POTR thrives on recommendations from existing customers!

Now that we have looked at the bones and flesh of the MMS, let's check out the skin! They say that your smile is the most beautiful part of your face. Let's see how SMIL can add beauty to our message!

Controlling Message Presentation

SMIL (Synchronized Multimedia Integration Language, pronounced "smile") is an XML-based HTML-like markup language. With SMIL, you can create slide-like presentations with text, images, streaming audio/video, and other media types. There are many standards and specifications about SMIL, as it has been around for quite some time. 3GPP (3rd Generation Partnership Program) has defined a SMIL profile for MMS. W3C's Mobile Profile is compatible with that. W3C has also defined SMIL Basic Profile and SMIL Extended Mobile Profile. For this book, we will only look at basic SMIL. You can get a lot more information from `http://www.w3.org/AudioVideo/`.

For starters, let's review the NMIT-generated SMIL:

```
<?xml version="1.0"?>
<!DOCTYPE smil PUBLIC "-//W3C//DTD SMIL 2.0//EN"
        "http://www.w3.org/2001/SMIL20/SMIL20.dtd">
<smil xmlns="http://www.w3.org/2001/SMIL20/Language">
 <head>
```

```
<layout>
<!-- This is a generated SMIL file.  -->
 <root-layout width="160" height="120" />
 <region id="Image" width="160" height="100" />
 <region id="Text" width="160" height="20" top="100" />
</layout>
</head>
 <body>
  <par>
    <img src="potr_logo.jpg" region="Image" />
  </par>
  <par>
    <text src="special_offer.txt" region="Text" />
  </par>
 </body>
</smil>
```

Understanding SMIL Elements

Let us review the elements of the SMIL code we just saw:

- The first three lines define the XML document type and the SMIL namespace—very similar to XHTML.

- The head element defines the layout of the presentation. There are two regions in our presentation, one for the image and the other for the text. The layout element also defines the size.

- The ID attribute in region is important. We must use the same ID in the img or text elements for the item to be placed in that region.

- The par element is as such a slide. Elements within a par element are run in parallel. In this case, we have only one element in each par element.

- img and text elements define the source of content. You can specify the Content-Location in the src. If you have used Content-Id's, you can specify something like "src=cid:contentid".

That was basic SMIL. Now let us see what are the other modules/elements in SMIL.

Modules and Elements of SMIL 2.1 Mobile Profile

The following table lists the ten modules and their elements of SMIL 2.1 Mobile Profile as described by W3C. As you can see, SMIL is very powerful. It allows you to apply transitions to slides, show content in parallel or sequence, define links, position regions on the screen, and even define metadata for your presentation.

Module	Elements
ContentControl	switch, prefetch
Layout	region, root-layout, layout, regPoint
LinkAnchor	a, area
MediaContent	text, img, audio, video, ref, textstream, param, paramGroup
Metainformation	meta, metadata
Structure	smil, head, body
Schedule	par, seq
Transition	transition

Transitions—that looks interesting. Why not add a transition to our special offer? Let's do that!

More SMIL: Applying Transitions

We can define a `transition` element in `head` and use it with content elements. Review the following code for a customization of our MMS message. We have broken it down into multiple slides, applied duration to them, and also applied in/out transitions to a few slides.

```
<smil>
  <head>
    <layout>
      <root-layout width="120" height="140"/>
      <region id="Image" width="120" height="80" left="0" top="0"/>
      <region id="Text" width="120" height="60" left="0" top="80"/>
    </layout>
    <transition id="wipeScreen" type="clockWipe" subtype="
                    clockwipeTwelve" dur="1s" scope="screen" />
  </head>
  <body>
    <par dur="3s">
      <img src="potr_logo.jpg" region="Image" />
      <text src="intro.txt" region="Text" transOut="wipeScreen" />
    </par>
    <par dur="5s">
      <img src="pizza_pepperoni_120.jpg" region="Image" />
      <text src="cid:special_offer.txt" region="Text" />
      </par>
      <par dur="3s">
          <img src="cid:pizza_pepperoni_120.jpg" region="Image" />
      <text src="discount.txt" region="Text" transIn="wipeScreen" />
```

```
        </par>
        <par dur="2s">
            <img src="potr_logo.jpg" region="Image" />
            <text src="thank_you.txt" region="Text" />
        </par>
    </body>
</smil>
```

That was easy to understand, wasn't it? Different elements and the transition applied via `transIn` or `transOut` attributes. The following screenshot shows how the slides will render, but without the screen wipe effect!

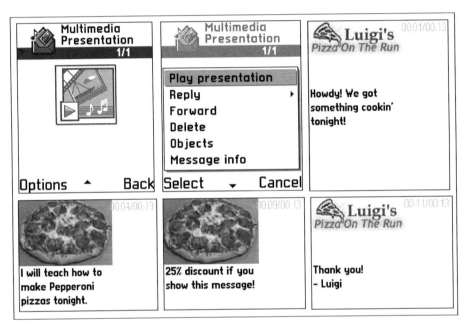

You can try out different SMIL elements and get your message to look the way you want. You may even use a SMIL editor to combine various media files you have designed. Test it on the device to make sure the SMIL doesn't make your device cry!

But hey, we haven't tried our message on a real mobile device yet! How about sending it out now?

Sending Multimedia Messages through Our Gateway

Sending an MMS message is similar to sending an SMS message at API level. Internally, an MMS message has to go through different stages before it finally gets delivered to the device. Let us start by sending our MMS message using our Clickatell gateway.

Time for Action: Sending MMS Messages via Clickatell

1. We first need to upload our MMS message to a publicly accessible URL so that the device can download it. Using an FTP program, we upload our `offer.mms` to the POTR server.

2. Now let's add a function to our SMSGateway class. This function will take all parameters and pass them to the Clickatell gateway. Notice that the API URL is different and we need to authenticate for sending the notification.

```
public function SendMMS($username, $password, $apiId, $to, $from,
                                      $subject, $mms_from, $mms_url)
{
    $to = $this->CleanUpPhoneNumber($to);
    if ($to == "")
    {
        return false;
    }
    // The API URL is slightly different for MMS
    $this->apiURL = "http://api.clickatell.com/mms/";
    // We also need to authenticate for this call
    $params['user'] = $username;
    $params['password'] = $password;
    $params['api_id'] = $apiId;
    $params['to'] = $to;
    $params['from'] = $from;
    $params['mms_subject'] = $subject;
    $params['mms_class'] = 82; // 80 (Personal), 81
    // (Advertisement), 82 (Informational), 83 (Auto)
    $params['mms_expire'] = 3000; // Expiry time in seconds
    $params['mms_from'] = $mms_from;
    $params['mms_url'] = $mms_url;
    $params['to'] = $to;
    $command = "ind_push.php";
    if ($this->Request($command, $params))
    {
        return true;
    }
}
```

3. We can now create a new PHP file to send out MMS messages using this function. The following code shows this file. We keep the subject, from, and MMS URL short, so that it can easily go in the WAP Push SMS. Unlike SMS, there is no specific limit on MMS message size though.

```php
<?php
$sms = new SMSGateway();
$mms_url = "http://potr.mehtanirav.com/mms/offer.mms";
$result = $sms->SendMMS("username", "password", "3015229",
        "919322504767", "919322504767", "25% discount,
        Pizza making", "Luigi - POTR", $mms_url);
if ($result)
{
    echo "MMS Notification sent!";
}
else
{
    echo "Could not send the notification.";
}
?>
```

4. We add "mms" to our `$validActions` array in `index.php`, and can now access the page. It should connect to Clickatell and send out the notification.

5. On the mobile, you will receive a notification asking to download/open the MMS message. Open the MMS message, and you can view our special offer with all its special effects!

How is an MMS Message Sent?

So how did you get the MMS Message? There are multiple stages in an MMS delivery. The following figure shows the overall transactions going on between the MMS originator (on left) and the MMS receiver (on the right).

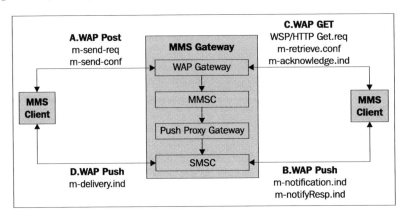

Let's review what's happening:

1. When you send an MMS Message request, a `m-send-req` Protocol Data Unit (PDU) is sent to the MMS Gateway over WAP Post. The gateway accepts the MMS for delivery and sends a confirmation back (`m-send-conf`).

2. Through a binary SMS known as WAP Push, the gateway sends a notification (`m-notification.ind`) to the receiver that a new MMS Message is available. The MMS client at the receiver end may opt to download the message later. In this case a `m-notifyResp.ind` message is sent back to the gateway. Essentially, the client is telling the gateway that "Oh yeah... I got your notification. But I will see the message later, I'm kinda busy right now!".

3. When the client is ready to see the message, (which could be immediately as well), it sends a request (`m-retrieve.conf` or `HTTP Get.req`) to the gateway. The gateway picks up the MMS Message, sends it over the client, and waits for the client to send `m-acknowledge.ind`.

4. Once the acknowledgement is received, the gateway passes back an `m-delivery.ind` message to the originator, saying "Hey, I've done my job. Your message is delivered!"

Don't you think MMS is much more involved than SMS? All those "m-*.*" PDUs can surely get confusing for the first few times! But hey, you don't need to bother about them until you want to get deeper into MMS delivery. Till then, you can be happy pushing messages through the Gateway API!

MMS Gateways do Good Work

Apart from pushing around those PDUs, a typical MMS Gateway does a whole lot of other things as well. It may convert media files in the MMS message to a format supported by the mobile device, route the MMS message to an email address, or forward it to another MMSC. Do check up the MMS services of the gateway you select. You never know when you will need that extra bit!

It's time to switch gears now. We have seen how to send multimedia messages, let's look at how we can receive them now.

Receiving Photos from Customers via MMS

An MMS message can be delivered to an email address, and that's the easiest way to receive MMS messages on a server! Simply ask the customers to use your email address in the To field of the MMS message, and the gateway will send over the MMS message to your email address. If the gateway is good (and most of them are), it will send the media files as attachments to the email. This means you can use a standard email parsing class to extract the attachments.

Many gateways can also receive MMS messages on your behalf. The user will send the MMS message to a particular number (could be a short code too), and the gateway will process the MMS message and send it to you as an email or POST it to a URL you specify. If your gateway provides such a feature, you can go ahead and use that.

If you are going to get the MMS message via email (either directly or via the gateway), you can use standard POP libraries to fetch the message along with the attachments. There are many such libraries available, so we won't cover them here. Let's look at how we can decode an actual MMS message for now. We will also not worry about getting the MMS message itself. We are assuming that's taken care of.

Openwave and Nokia have good sets of libraries in Java and C++ to decode MMS. There are other sources too. When it comes to PHP, there aren't really many options. Jonathan Heyman's MMSDecoder (http://heyman.info/mmsdecoder.php) is a very good library to decode MMS messages. His code extends the work of Stefan Hellkvist's MMSLib code (http://hellkvist.org/software/).

 You can use MMSLib to create MMS messages through a script—including text and images at run time.

Time for Action: Decoding an MMS Message

1. Download and extract the MMS Decoder library to the POTR web directory. The heart of the library is a file called mmsdecoder.php. Open the file and turn on debugging by defining the DEBUG constant as 1 near the start of the file.

2. Create a new file—decodeMMS.inc.php—and include the mmsdecoder. php file. Then let's decode user.mms—an MMS file we have got. Calling the parse() method on the decode will process the MMS message and create different parts for the content in it. The code for this would look like:

```
require_once("mmsdecoder.php");
$mmsFile = "user.mms";
```

```
$mmsData = file_get_contents($mmsFile);
$mms = new MMSDecoder($mmsData);
$mms->parse();
```

3. Luigi wants to put up photos of his customers eating his pizzas along with their testimonials! So we are looking for a photo and a text in the MMS message. We can loop through the message parts, check the content type of each part, and save the photo if it is an image. As we are looking for only one image and one text data section, we can skip processing the other parts once we have got them. Following code achieves this:

```
$photoFile = $messageText = "";
foreach($mms->PARTS as $mmsPart)
{
    $type = $mmsPart->CONTENTTYPE;
    // Check if this is an image type data
    if ($photoFile == "" && eregi("jpg|jpeg|gif|png", $type))
    {
        $ext = substr($type, strrpos($type, "/")+1);
        $photoFile = time().".$ext";
        $mmsPart->save($photoFile);
    }
    // Check if this is a plain text data,
    // we don't want any other type of text
    if ($messageText == "" && eregi("plain", $type))
    {
        $messageText = $mmsPart->DATA;
    }
    // If we got both files, we can save the info
    // and complete the task!
    if ($photoFile != "" && $messageText != "")
    {
        $info['from'] = $mms->FROM;
        $info['subject'] = $mms->SUBJECT;
        $info['photo'] = $photoFile;
        $info['message'] = $messageText;
        // Code to save to DB
        echo "<p>Saved the new message</p>";
        print_r($info); // For debugging only!
        break;
    }
}
```

4. When we execute the code now, it will pick up the `user.mms` message, process it, and show us the from and subject headers, and the message. The photo file would have been saved as `somenumber.jpg`, where the number is actually the UNIX Timestamp of when we processed the message.

5. We can save the information in a database and display it to our visitors in a special "You Said It!" section!

What Just Happened: Decoding the MMS Message

The MMSDecoder class checks the message data—processing all the headers and their values. After it has processed all headers, it checks the content type of the message—multipart related or multipart mixed, and handles the parts accordingly. The library includes an `MMSPart` class that stores data of each part.

Each part has a content type. We check that and save it if it's an image. We store the saved image name in a variable, so that we can skip processing other images in the message. If you want to save all images from a message, you can use an array to store all image file names and append a counter variable to the name to ensure they don't get overwritten.

We take the first text message into a variable, and save it to the table directly. We have not implemented database operations here, but they are easy to add.

Note that the library does not yet support getting the name of the file in MMS. If you want to know the name of the media file, you will have to hack the decode code yourself! You can also check for a SMIL file in the message, and guess file names based on the SMIL file data.

For now, it is sufficient to get the file contents!

MMS's Potential is Yet to Be Exploited!

Multimedia Messaging Service really opens up new doors for mobile web developers. It allows you to send rich content to your subscribers effortlessly. You can send market alerts with graphs to your customers, or best contributed videos of the day or a clip of the latest song of their favorite band.

The full potential of MMS is yet to be exploited. The ability to receive an MMS as email allows you to connect to your mobile customers right away. The stage is set; all we need is a killer MMS app!

Luigi, on the other hand, is not interested in developing the next killer app on MMS. He is worried about how he can deliver a delicious pizza to his next customer! Let's round up what we learned in this chapter.

Summary

In this chapter, we learned to send and receive MMS messages. Specifically:

- We created an MMS message with Nokia's Mobile Internet Toolkit and previewed it in the Content Authoring SDK.

- We learned about SMIL, the different elements, and how they can be used to create slide-like presentations with transition effects.

- We sent out the MMS message using our gateway.

- We got a taste of the inner workings of MMS delivery and the multipart structure of MMS messages.

- We used the MMSDecoder class to decode a received message and extract a photo and text from it.

Luigi wants to target both MMS and SMS users. He is already sending out SMS messages, but now wants to receive order delivery confirmations from customers. This will allow him to track the exact time taken in the delivery! In the next chapter, we will learn how to receive text messages.

8
Making Money via Mobile Devices

Mobile Payment is a hot topic today. People talk about billions of dollars of market opportunities: Micro and Macro payments via mobile devices, and even using the mobile as an e-wallet. Staying on the cutting edge of technology, Luigi too wants to explore new opportunities of growth for Pizza On The Run via mobile commerce.

We will explore and set up a mobile payment system for POTR in this chapter. Specifically, we will look at:

- Getting money through PayPal
- Evaluating Mobile Payment Methods, their pros and cons
- Security Concerns in Mobile Payments
- Using SMS in Mobile Payment, Premium SMS, and Short Codes
- Receiving Text Messages via a short code

Everyone wants to make money! And we want it fast! So let us get straight to getting money!

Getting Money through PayPal

PayPal (www.paypal.com) is one of the largest online payment gateways. Its Mobile Checkout feature allows us to get paid via mobile devices. The process is similar to getting payments on the Web, and is easy to integrate. There are different methods of getting payment via mobile devices and many mobile payment gateways too. Later in this chapter, we will evaluate these options, but Luigi already has a PayPal account, so for now, let's see how we can integrate PayPal Mobile Checkout for POTR. The first step is configure our PayPal account for mobile payments.

Time for Action: Setting Up the PayPal Account for Mobile Payments

1. For Mobile Checkout to work, you must have a Business Account with PayPal. So if you have a Personal or Premier account, upgrade to Business account. Note that if your account is not verified, it may take a few days. If you don't have a PayPal account, you can easily register one at www.paypal.com.

2. Next, log in to your PayPal account. Go to **Profile**, and **API Settings**. Register a new API username, password, and key. This sets the credentials, using which our application will access PayPal.

3. Once you have the API key, go to the **Grant Permissions** option and "View/edit permissions". Enter the API username and check "SetMobileCheckout" and "DoMobileCheckoutPayment" options from the list. We will use these two methods for mobile checkout integration.

4. You will see a confirmation screen as shown in the following screenshot. Confirm by clicking on the button that says **Give Permission**.

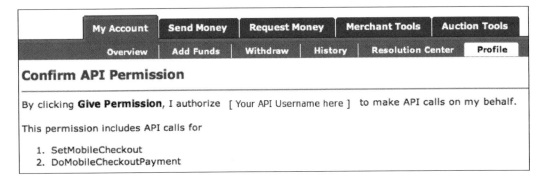

5. We are now set to integrate with PayPal!

Why This Configuration?

PayPal has excellent security mechanisms. Setting up an API key and permissions on it allows us to manage our e-commerce stores better. We can grant different levels of permissions to different API keys. When we pass the API key and user information to PayPal, it will allow access based on this configuration. Without this configuration, we won't be able to use Mobile Checkout either. But now that we have configured our account, let us see how to integrate PayPal in our code.

Mobile Checkout is a Three-Step Flow

Once the customer has ordered her or his pizza, we want to give her or him an option to make a payment via PayPal. We will pass the order information to PayPal and update the order status once the payment is received. As we configured, we need to make two calls to PayPal: SetMobileCheckout and DoMobileCheckoutPayment.

1. SetMobileCheckout: This call sets the order information with PayPal. We pass order amount, currency, return and cancel URLs, custom variables, etc. to this call. A successful call returns a string token that we need to use in all further calls for this order.

2. In the second step, the customer is redirected to PayPal where she or he will enter her or his payment information—credit card details or PayPal account information.

3. DoMobileCheckoutPayment: This is the call that actually gets the funds to our PayPal account. Without this call, money will not get to our account!

PayPal provides an SDK that we can use for integration. The PHP SDK comes with sample code to call PayPal APIs and other useful functionality. You can download it from `http://www.paypal.com/IntegrationCenter/ic_downloads.html`. Now, let us use this SDK and add some of our code to do the integration.

Time for Action: Integrating PayPal Mobile Checkout with POTR

1. The last step in the POTR order process—`order_step4.inc.php`—saves the order information to a database table and shows a success message to the customer. Let us add a link on this page to make payment via PayPal. The following code does this:

```
if ($orderObj->Save())
{
    echo "<wall:h2>Order Placed!</wall:h2>";
    echo $orderObj;
    echo "<p>Your order is placed.</p>";
    echo "<p><a href=\"?action=payment&id=".$orderObj->id."\"
                                    >Pay via Paypal</a>!</p>";
    $_SESSION["orderInfo"] = null;
}
```

2. Next, we create a `payment.inc.php` page, and add it to `$validActions` array in `index.php`.

3. We have combined the `constants.php` and `CallerService.php` files of the PayPal PHP SDK into a single file that we will use: `paypal.lib.php`. This will make it easier for us to integrate later. Note that we need cURL extension of PHP installed to use this SDK. The following code shows the structure of `paypal.lib.php`:

```php
<?php
if($sandbox)
{
  // sandbox (testing) authentication information
  define('API_USERNAME', 'sdk-three_api1.sdk.com');
  define('API_PASSWORD', 'QFZCWN5HZM8VBG7Q');
  define('API_SIGNATURE',
         'A-IzJhZZjhg29XQ2qnhapuwxIDzyAZQ92FRP5dqBzVesOkzbdUONzmOU');
  define('API_ENDPOINT', 'https://api-3t.sandbox.paypal.com/nvp');
  define('PAYPAL_URL', 'https://www.sandbox.paypal.com/wc?t=');
}
else
{
  // production authentication information
  // similar to above...
}
define('VERSION', '3.0');
// Use cURL and make a request to PayPal for $methodName
// Pass $nvpStr (Name Value Pair) as parameters in the request
// Also pass the API authentication information
// Check the result and use deformatNVP() to convert
// it to an array and return
function hash_call($methodName,$nvpStr)
{
    // implementation skipped...
}
// Convert the response string name value pairs into an array
function deformatNVP($nvpstr)
{
    // implementation skipped...
}
?>
```

4. Let us start building our `payment.inc.php` file now. The following code shows the structure of the file. We handle both calls to PayPal and return values from PayPal in this file.

```php
<?php
$sandbox = true;
include('classes/paypal.lib.php');
// If we got order ID, but no token, it means we have to start
```

```php
// payment process with PayPal
if (isset($_REQUEST['id']) && !isset($_REQUEST['token']))
{
    // Load all order information
    // Pass on order information to PayPal
    // If we get the token, pass the user on
}
// Got return from PayPal
else if (isset($_REQUEST['token']))
{
    if ($_REQUEST['mode'] == 'return')
    {
        // Done well, now complete the transaction and
        //                                     get the funds!
    }
    else
    {
        echo '<p>Order was cancelled.</p>';
    }
}
else
{
    echo '<p>Invalid parameters. Please try again!</p>';
}
?>
```

5. Once we have loaded all the order information in `$orderObj`, we can pass it to PayPal and call SetMobileCheckout. In the example here, we are passing only a few details, but you can pass all the details you want. The return URLs have to be publicly accessible when you put this online.

```php
// Pass on order information to PayPal
$param['AMT']          = $orderObj->total;
$param['CURRENCYCODE'] = 'USD';
$param['DESC']         = $orderObj->GetSummary(); // Order description
$baseURL = 'http://'.$_SERVER['HTTP_HOST'].$_SERVER[
                                    'REQUEST_URI'].'&mode=';
$param['RETURNURL']= $baseURL.'return';
$param['CANCELURL']= $baseURL.'cancel';
$param['INVNUM']= $orderObj->id;
$param['PHONENUM']= $orderObj->phone;
$param['CUSTOM']= session_id(); // Any custom data can be sent
$request = '';
foreach($param as $key=>$value)
```

```
{
    $request .= "&$key=".urlencode($value);
}
// perform the api callback for SetMobileCheckout with
//                                             those values
$result = hash_call('SetMobileCheckout',$request);
// If we get success, redirect the user to PayPal
if(strtoupper($result['ACK']) == 'SUCCESS')
{
    header('Location: '.PAYPAL_URL.urldecode($result['TOKEN']));
}
else
{
    // No token, call failed!
    echo "<p><b>Could not initialize PayPal connection.</b><
                        /p><p>".print_r($result, true)."</p>";
}
```

6. PayPal will redirect the user to the return or cancel URL once the payment is done. We are using the mode variable to determine if it was a return or cancel operation. Based on these values, we can update the order status or show a failure message to the user. The following code shows our implementation.

```
// Done well, now complete the transaction and get the funds!
$result = hash_call('DoMobileCheckoutPayment',
                            '&token='.$_REQUEST['token']);
if (strtoupper($result['ACK']) == 'SUCCESS')
{
    // Order successful, we can update it now
    $orderObj = new Order(null, null);
    // We can process/validate all returned info here...
    $orderObj->id = $_REQUEST['INVNUM'];
    $orderObj->UpdateStatus('P');
    echo '<p>Payment successful. The order will soon be
                                    processed.</p>';
}
```

7. At this stage, we can customize the APIError.php file that comes in PayPal SDK to format the errors the way we want to show them. We can also specify another file to handle errors in our paypal.lib.php file.

8. That's all! We are set with PayPal integration now. The following figure shows how a customer may experience this process.

How Does This Work?

As depicted in the previous figure, the customer is redirected to PayPal after we get the token. Here, she can login with her PayPal email and password. If she or he has used PayPal for mobile payments earlier, and activated her mobile number, she can login with the mobile number and PIN only. If not, she gets the option to set them up in the next screen. She or he can then review the payment information and make payment. If the customer does not have a PayPal account, she or he can still pay using a credit card or bank account without needing to log in. PayPal sends an SMS confirmation to activate the phone number.

Once the payment is done, the user is brought back to merchant site (POTR), and we can validate the information received to show a confirmation message.

This process is similar to standard web checkout systems, and customers are receptive to it. The money gets debited from their Paypal account or credit card. The merchant gets the money in his or her PayPal account and can use the standard withdrawal process to get it to his or her bank account.

Alright, so we've got PayPal working. But what if we did not want to use PayPal? Well, there are many alternatives to PayPal! Google Checkout has started a mobile version. Bango (`www.bango.com`), Obopay (`www.obopay.com`), and mBlox (`www.mblox.com`) are leading companies that specialize in payments through mobile devices. Not only that, there are different ways to get paid too! What we developed so far is payment using credit cards over the mobile web. We can also use Premium SMS, direct billing, or proximity-based technologies. Let's review these options in bit more detail now.

Evaluating Mobile Payment Methods

The first step in evaluating mobile payment methods is to understand the context. What is it that a customer will buy using a mobile device? Of course, mobile payment is a huge potential market. People who have not made a single transaction on the Internet are paying good money for Premium SMS-based services. Customers do not mind paying for a wallpaper or ringtone using their mobile phones. The resistance increases as the price of the goods go higher.

When we begin to choose a mobile payment method, we must understand the customer demographics and behavior. The method may vary depending on the services we are providing too—wallpapers, ringtones, games, movie tickets, contest voting, clothes, and other goods, or pizzas! We will also need to consider their location. For some countries, we may be left with only one option of payment, for others, we may have many.

Once we have figured out the requirements, making a technical choice is easier. Here are the most common options for mobile payment:

Premium SMS

SMS messages that are charged higher than normal are the most popular mechanism to get money from customers today. A user will send a text message to a special number. The network operator will pass on the message to the content provider/ your application. Your application will then deliver the content to the user. Content may be sent over a WAP Push or any other mechanism. The network operator keeps most of the money (50% to 60%) and the rest goes to the content provider. After deducting service charges and taxes, the content provider is typically left with about 20% of the pie.

Pros and Cons

- Most widely used approach for micro payments.

- Network operator manages billing and records. The merchant's job is to provide content/goods.

- Customers are accustomed to this method, both in pre-paid and post-paid subscription schemes.

- The biggest drawback is the share left with the merchant. The only way to make money here is to have more customers. A bigger pie will make your piece bigger too!

- There may be many implementation aspects involved — starting from the networks to support, to ensuring the content gets delivered to the customers.

WAP-Based Credit Card Payment

Customers with WAP-capable mobile devices can pay through the mobile web. The service provider (we, the merchant) uses an online payment gateway. Customers enter their credit card information through the mobile device and that gets charged. Many specialized gateways offer mobile phone and PIN number-based authentication to simplify the process for customers. The payment can also be initialized by sending a WAP Push message to the customer, opening which will automatically take them to the payment page.

Pros and Cons

- Extends the already available infrastructure of web-based payments.

- WAP Payments are more secure and provide integration flexibility to the merchant.

- The content provider can determine whether content will be supported on the customer's handset or not and sell an appropriate version.

- The merchant is not tied to network operators.

- The goods or services provided may be anything — not just something the customer will consume on her or his mobile device.

- The biggest difficulty in this system is that only users who are comfortable using a mobile browser would use this method.

- Payment gateways can get very expensive for micro payments.

- If the customer does not have a credit card or WAP access, she or he is out of our reach then!

- Network operators do not like this method as it bypasses them!

Direct Billing

It is much easier to add charges for what customers purchased on their mobile phone bills. Like the Premium SMS system, this method uses the network operators' existing billing system to charge and manage the transactions. Customers can get itemized bills like those for credit cards. Financial institutions (banks or credit card companies) and network operators cooperate to make this happen. The customer would enter her or his authentication information on a website (or some other mechanism) and the charges for the purchase will show up in her or his mobile bill statement. Pre-paid customers will have the charges deducted from their balance right away.

Pros and Cons

- Direct Billing covers most customers and removes the complexity of sending messages around for billing.
- This also makes it less expensive than other methods.
- Direct Billing is very flexible in terms of charges, discounts, and billing. Customers too get itemized bills to show the exact details of the charges and the goods they bought.
- Direct Billing is still not mainstream. Not all operators support it.

Proximity Payment

Proximity Transaction via mobile devices is an interesting method, though not very popular in the mobile web. The mobile device has a special chip or software/hardware extension that allows it to communicate with the point-of-sale system. When the customer goes to the cashier or the POS, the POS and mobile device communicate with each other, the customer gets a notification on her or his device, confirms the transaction, and the charge goes through. The communication may happen over Bluetooth, Infrared, WiFi, RFID, or other carrier. It may also happen over USSD (Unstructured Supplementary Services Data)—a protocol similar to SMS, but with real-time connection and special features for financial needs.

Pros and Cons

- This method can be used for a variety of needs— both micro and macro payments. It can also be used for unattended POS like parking booths.
- This is a secure method of payment. The customer is physically close to the point-of-sale system, which creates more confidence.
- The method requires special software/hardware to be available. This limits its reach and feasibility.

- Proximity payment can be a good subsidiary payment mechanism for the mobile web, but may not be mainstream. E.g. a PIN/barcode can be generated on the mobile web for a rock concert, and customer will pay for the ticket while she or he parks the car.

Service Credits, Prepaid Cards, Embedded Smart Cards, and Interactive Voice Response (IVR)-based systems are some other alternatives available for mobile payment.

Apart from technical and user needs, you should also consider security aspects of the payment mechanism you choose. It's easy to steal a mobile phone or hijack Bluetooth data transmission. Let's get some perspective on what can go wrong in mobile payments.

Security Concerns in Mobile Payments

Here's a quick list of possible attacks in mobile payments. Knowing what can go wrong allows you to protect against it!

- A mobile device can be infected by a virus. This virus can then capture sensitive information, including data being transmitted during credit card-based transactions.

- A mobile device can be stolen. The track of transactions through Premium SMS can be easily found, and new transactions can be made before service deactivation.

- Typical PINs are 4 digit long. Once the attacker knows the phone number of a person, he or she can try to guess the PIN!

- An average mobile user is not an expert on technology or security. She or he may keep credit card information in plain text on the device itself, or give out information to anyone else.

- Data can be hijacked on the network, over the air, or between the merchant and the payment gateway, and can be changed and retransmitted.

- It is easy to spoof SMS. Spoofed SMS messages can be sent to the payment gateway for confirming a payment.

Mobile Payment Forum (`www.mobilepaymentforum.org`) has some excellent white papers on security and best practices for mobile payment. Going through them will give you a concrete understanding of the threats and possible solutions for each.

We have now reviewed the different options available for mobile payment. We have also seen how to use a WAP-based mobile payment system. Let us now turn to SMS. How can we use SMS for mobile payment?

Using SMS in Mobile Payment

Almost all the wallpaper and ringtone providers are running on Premium SMS-based payments. Even the votes we cast using SMS on a television contest are charged higher than normal. The following figure illustrates how SMS can be used to place an order.

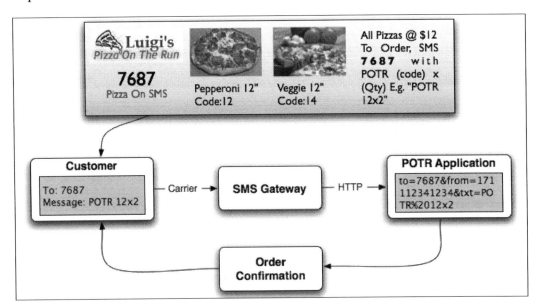

There are a few important aspects of this flow.

- POTR will advertise pizzas in newspapers, television, or any other media. Along with product information, we will also put up a code.

- To order, the customer has to send a message to a special number (called the Short Code) with a message in a specific format.

- The Short Code may be shared by many service providers, and hence the message may contain a keyword that will determine that it's meant for POTR.

- Along with the keyword, it will also have order information. The item code and quantity in our case.

- The network operator will deliver the message to the SMS Gateway, or Short Code Service Provider.

- The SMS Gateway will make an HTTP GET/POST request to POTR and pass on the entire message, along with the sender information.

- POTR can now process the order the way it wants. In our case, Luigi'll call back and confirm the order and take the address of the customer!

- The customer is charged a premium fee for sending the message. POTR gets charged for SMS Gateway services and short code provisioning.

- POTR also takes care of order fulfillment. The customer will get a hot pizza in the next half an hour!

Let's look closer at two components of this flow: Receiving Messages and Short Codes.

Receiving Text Messages

We have seen how we can send messages using an SMS Gateway in Chapter 6. The process is as simple as making an HTTP request to the gateway-provided URL with certain parameters. But when we want to receive text messages, the job gets a little complicated.

To receive messages, we need a number that people can send messages to and then, a system that will receive and read messages sent to that number. The final step in the process is to forward the message to our application via an HTTP request. The critical part in this process is the number that people can send messages to. We need to buy such a number from the SMS gateway and pay a monthly fee to keep it alive.

Such a number will normally be the full 12 to 16 digit mobile number. Some services can also use a "tagged number". A tagged number is an actual mobile number with some additional digits added at the end. All messages sent to the actual mobile number, irrespective of the tagged digits, will come to that number. The gateway can then route the message to the appropriate account based on the tagged numbers we have purchased.

But Luigi thinks this number is too long! And he wants to get a Short Code!

Getting a Short Code

A short code is like a domain name—an easy-to-remember number that will be used to access applications online. Luigi, like many others, wants to map the short code to POTR—and wants to buy 7687 as his short code. A short code is constant across all network operators in the region (typically a continent). So all mobile users can send a message to the same short code and we will be able to receive them.

The process of getting a short code can be time consuming—Clickatell takes up to 90 days. For the US and the UK, you can register short codes from http://www.usshortcodes.com (US) or http://www.short-codes.com (UK). Other countries have their own process of acquiring a short code.

Even short codes have two types: Random or Vanity. Vanity short codes are easier-to-remember codes that are sold at a premium price. Random short codes are random 4-6 digit numbers. The charges for both random or vanity short codes vary for different continents.

Assuming we have got the 7687 short code for POTR, let us see how we can receive messages to it! Not all SMS gateways offer such a two-way messaging facility, but Clickatell has it. So let's get going!

Receiving Messages via Clickatell

1. The first step is to activate two-way messaging on our account. We then buy the short code and wait for it to function. In the meanwhile, we can go ahead and do our integration code. Refer to `http://www.clickatell.com/products/two_way.php` for more details on two-way messaging activation with Clickatell.

2. To receive messages via HTTP, we must set up a callback URL with our API. We set this up from our Clickatell Central account.

3. Our callback URL will point to `receiveMessage.inc.php`—a new file we are creating. In the file, we first validate incoming parameters from Clickatell. Let's see how this bit looks in the file.

```php
<?php
// Clickatell sends us following parameters
$from = $_REQUEST['from'];
$to = $_REQUEST['to'];
$timestamp = $_REQUEST['timestamp'];
$text = $_REQUEST['text'];
if ($from == "" || $to == "" || $timestamp == "" || $text == "")
{
    echo "<p>Invalid parameters.</p>";
    return;
}
?>
```

4. We can now split the text into order parameters then loop over them and add items to the order. The following code shows the structure of this part, added right after the previous code.

```php
// Process the message here
// Message format is "POTR (Item Code)x(Qty)"
// Push a space around x so that we can split at space later
$text = str_replace('x', ' x ', $text);
// Convert all double spaces into single spaces
while(ereg('  ', $text))
```

```
{
    $text = str_replace('  ', ' ', $text);
}
$text = strtoupper(trim($text));
// Now we can split at space to get order parameters
$params = explode(' ', $text);
$identifier = array_shift($params);
if ($identifier != 'POTR')
{
    echo "<p>Invalid command.!</p>";
}
for($i = 0; $i < count($params); $i = $i + 3)
{
    $itemCode = $params[$i];
    $qty = $params[$i+2];
    // Validate the itemCode and qty here
    // Add to order
}
// Save the order and notify customer
```

5. We now have a basic structure ready for processing incoming messages! We do not need to show any output here, because the request will come from Clickatell.

Sending Messages That Can Be Replied To

Clickatell needs an additional parameter while sending messages to make sure they can be replied to. This parameter is called "MO" (Mobile Originated) and the value for that must be 1. When we pass this parameter, Clickatell will set the number in the "from" parameter as the one that users can reply to. It will also try to route the message through an appropriate network operator. When the user replies to the message, Clickatell can pick it up and route it to our application. This completes the two-way messaging for us!

So far, we have seen many advanced methods of receiving payments via mobile devices. But some payment gateways make it absolutely easy to get payments via SMS! Just send an SMS like "send 5 to orders@potr.com"! Sounds interesting? Let's find out more!

Making it Easier—Payment Gateways Help get More Money!

We mentioned that you have a good choice of mobile payment gateways. Many of these gateways support more than one method to get mobile payments. For example, Obopay (among others) makes it absolutely easy to send money to someone. You can send an SMS to 62729 (in the US) like "send 6505551212 17.95 Pepperoni Pizza plus Coke" (see the following figure). The money will then be sent to the user with mobile phone number 6505551212. If the owner of that number does not have an Obopay account, she or he will get an SMS notification and can sign up to receive money.

Obopay allows payments via WAP, and also special software that you can download and install on your phone. PayPal too has a "Text 2 Buy" service that allows sending money with a simple message.

Bango on the other hand, specializes in digital goods under $10. It covers a lot of regions of the world. And it also complies to Payforit (http://www.short-codes. com/payforit/)—a payment service supported by all UK mobile network operators. Bango also provides extensive reports and search integration.

Different mobile payment gateways may offer different features. But the cost is also a major factor to consider. Consider all the costs involved when you decide on the payment gateway—including short code charges.

We now have a good foundation in mobile payment. Let's review what we learned in this chapter.

Summary

In this chapter, we learned to receive payments and messages via devices. Specifically we looked at:

- Using SetMobileCheckout and DoMobileCheckoutPayment for payment through PayPal
- Premium SMS, Credit Card, Proximity Payments, and other methods of Mobile Payment, their pros and cons
- An overview of security concerns in Mobile Payments
- Receiving Text Messages via Clickatell
- The usage of short codes and how to obtain one

Luigi now wants an automated system to process orders coming via phone: an interactive voice response system that can give order status updates to customers and even take orders! Let's do some talking in the next chapter then!

9

Interactive Voice

Call in 1-800-POTR-NOW. Luigi greets you. He asks you the kind of pizza you want to order, the size, crust, and toppings you want. He confirms the order and takes your address, giving a promise to deliver the pizza within half an hour. You finish the call and wait for the fresh, hot, and delicious pizza to arrive!

Luigi has been doing this for years now. He loves to talk to the customers, but it gets too much sometimes! He has now come to us to find an alternative. He says, "How about a computer answering the call and taking the order?"

Hmm, that's an interesting challenge! Let us explore and develop an interactive voice response (IVR) system for Luigi in this chapter. Specifically, we will look at:

- Setting up an interactive voice response platform
- Playing pre-recorded audio and text to speech
- Accepting keypad inputs
- Accepting voice input and doing speech recognition
- Performing dynamic calculations on input
- Integrating with server-side scripting

Voice-driven systems bring a wealth of opportunities. Unlike a few years ago, it is possible now to do complex speech recognition. If you had to build an interactive voice based system earlier, you had to know arcane details about the hardware and network you were deploying on. Now, with standards-based languages, the job is much easier.

Let's get on and discover how easily we can build a sophisticated voice-driven ordering system for Luigi.

First, Some Basics

You wouldn't want to jump off a plane without parachute, right? So how can we get to the implementation without knowing some fundamentals? The following figure shows how a typical IVR application may function.

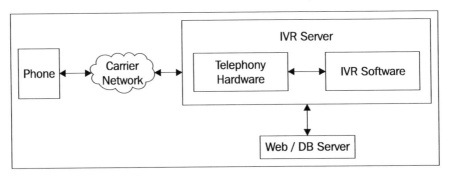

The user calls in using any network or device. The call arrives on the IVR server. Telephony hardware sitting on the server passes on this call to the IVR software. The IVR software processes the call—prompting the caller and accepting input via the keypad or voice. These inputs define the flow of the call. The IVR software optionally talks to a web or database server to dynamically retrieve or store information. Once the application work is finished, the call completes.

If only it was that easy! We must bust some jargon before we can get deeper into these systems!

Busting Some Jargon

As with any technology, IVR is full of its own jargon. Let's first understand it:

- VoiceXML (VXML): This is an XML-based language to develop voice-based applications. There are other options available, but W3C's VoiceXML is becoming the standard. VoiceXML has elements similar to XHTML, and works much like a form a customer is filling out. The only difference is that the form is being filled over a phone call in VoiceXML.

- CCXML: Call Control XML allows sophisticated call routing and conferencing. CCXML can be used in conjunction with VoiceXML.

- grXML: Grammar XML allows the speech recognition engine to identify what was spoken. grXML rules determine valid input for your applications.

- VoIP: Voice over IP is a protocol to transmit voice over standard IP networks. Skype and all other voice messengers use VoIP. And if you are wondering how VoIP relates to IVR, well, you can set up an IVR application that works over VoIP and you wouldn't need phone lines. People can call in using their VoIP software and you won't even touch the telecom networks!

- SIP: Session Initiation Protocol is a way to make Voice over IP (VoIP) calls. SIP is used extensively in VoIP applications to establish calls.

- DTMF: Dual Tone Multi-Frequency, or "touch tone", input means input via the phone's numeric keypad.

- Text To Speech (TTS): Converting a text to audio. There are many text-to-speech engines available, and different voices too — e.g. Male and Female.

- Speech Recognition: The process of understanding spoken words and converting them to text. For IVR applications, it's best to limit speech recognition to a few words per input.

IVR Infrastructure: Hosted or Owned?

The easiest way to run a voice application is to find a company that hosts VoiceXML-based IVR applications. It will also give you a number that customers can call to access your application. There are many service providers in this space and you can go for the best in your location. You can find some on Ken Rehor's World of VoiceXML page (`http://www.kenrehor.com/voicexml/`).

Alternatively, you can also set up your own server. You can get a VoiceXML platform and hook up a few telephone lines to it via supported interfaces. You can even get a VoiceXML plugin for your existing PBX system if you are using Asterisk (`www.asterisk.org`) or similar PBX software.

For our exploration, we will use Voxeo's Prophecy Server (`www.voxeo.com`). Prophecy is a free download, and is free to use for up to two simultaneous connections. It's standards compliant, and Voxeo also provides hosting. On top of that, Prophecy comes with a great speech recognition engine, VoiceXML development tools, and a helpful community! The whole deal is too good to be true!

Time for Action: Setting Up an Interactive Voice Response Platform

1. Download Prophecy from `www.voxeo.com`, and install it on your machine. For starters, the "small TTS" version is good.

2. Once it's running, you will get a Voxeo icon in your system tray. Select **Prophecy Home** option from there. Go to admin, and get a license key for your setup. This routine will take you to Voxeo's site. You can take the free 2-port license, and it will get set up automatically.

3. Now go to the Voxeo menu in the system tray and open **Log Viewer**. This opens up a console that's indispensable for debugging voice applications! The messages in the log viewer may not make sense right now, but that's OK! The following screenshot shows how the Log Viewer looks.

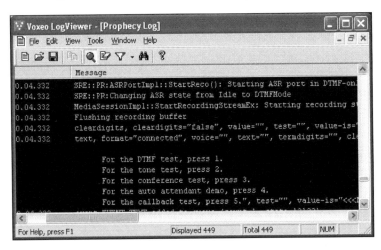

4. Now, open the **SIP Phone** from the Voxeo system tray menu. That should bring up a screen like the one shown in the following screenshot. This is the phone we will use to test our applications! To get an experience of how voice applications work, click on the **Dial** button. You will be greeted by the default Voxeo application, and from there you can perform a few basic tests—DTMF detection, auto attendant, conferencing, call back, etc. Go ahead and try them to ensure everything is set up correctly!

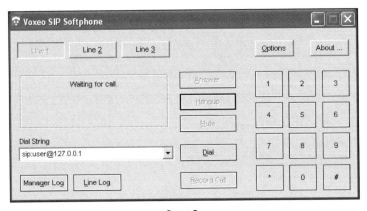

5. At this time, you can also look at the various tools in the **Prophecy Home**. There is a VoiceXML designer and tools to hook up your application with VoIP service providers. But we are ready with our platform now.

Getting Curious?

If you tried that sample Voxeo application, you will be curious about how things are working. The SIP Phone is a software phone. It uses SIP protocol to make calls to the Prophecy server. Prophecy's services are waiting for a call. Once the call comes in, they look up the location of the file that handles the call—just like how a web server would process a request. The file is loaded, processed, and audio output delivered to the caller.

Examining the Log Viewer will tell you a lot about the internals, how different parts of the Prophecy server work together and how they process user input.

We have got a taste of voice applications, now. Let's start writing our own Pizza Ordering application!

Designing the Call Flow of Our Application

Just as we need to take care of usability in our mobile web applications, we need to take care of it in our voice applications as well—in fact, more so in a voice application. Customers do not like to talk to machines, and when they do, they simply want to get their job done fast. If the machine cannot understand them, their frustration will increase. Customers also don't want to go through an endless chain of questions and number punching. Recall your experience calling a customer support number.

That's pretty much how our clients will feel about our application if we don't plan well!

Some principles we can follow in our applications are:

- Keep it short and simple.
- Don't let the user feel the machine is more intelligent than her or him.
- Don't have questions whose response the application can't understand.
- Test with real users, in real conditions!

Considering all that, let's put together a simple call flow for POTR. The following figure shows this flow. Notice that we have removed the side dish selection, and selecting different types of pizzas in this flow. We are also not taking the customer's address yet. We can add all that later.

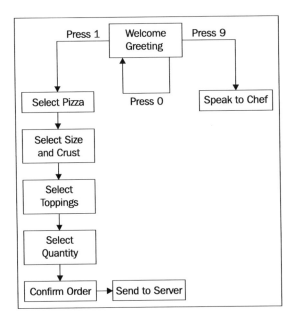

The first step is to welcome the caller. Time for some music!

Creating an Application to Play Audio

We want to greet our customers with a nice welcome message. They are used to hearing Luigi's voice, so we want them to continue with that. Yes, we were talking about Luigi's voice when we mentioned music! Here are the steps to build our first IVR application that plays Luigi's welcome greeting!

Time for Action: Creating an Application and Welcoming Callers

1. Using voice recording software (such as Sound Recorder on Windows), create a short welcome greeting. Save the file in 8bit, 8kHz u-law format as `welcome.wav`. Most servers will play back audio in this format, even if you save it in higher quality, so it's best to save in 8/8 format at the beginning. We have recorded Luigi's voice and saved the file!

2. Voxeo applications are stored in the `Program Files\Voxeo\www` folder by default. Locate the folder on your computer and create a new folder in it. Name it `potr`.

3. Copy the `welcome.wav` file to the `potr` folder we just created.

4. Create a new text file in this folder. Name it `index.xml`, and enter the following code in the file.

```xml
<?xml version="1.0" encoding="UTF-8"?>
<vxml version = "2.1">
<meta name="maintainer" content="youremail@yourdomain.com"/>
<form id="main">
<block>
  <audio src="welcome.wav">
  Welcome to Pizza On The Run.
  </audio>
</block>
</form>
</vxml>
```

5. Go to Prophecy Home—Administration. Then Call Routing. Change the route 1 to point to our application. Set the **Route ID** as `potr`, **Route Type** as VXML, and the **Route URL** as `http://127.0.0.1:9990/potr/index.xml`. The following screenshot shows how you can do it. Once they are changed, go to the bottom of the page and save the settings.

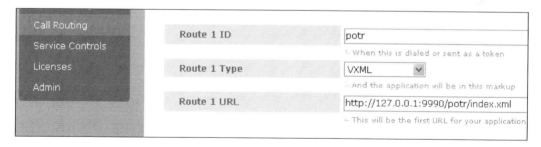

6. Go to SIP Phone now, and dial **sip:potr@127.0.0.1**. You should be greeted by your audio recording!

How Did This Work?

127.0.0.1 is the IP address of the local computer. So we are telling the phone to call an account named `potr` on this computer. Since we created a route for `potr` earlier, Prophecy will know that it has to process the VXML file at the given URL in response to this call. It will look up that file next.

The `index.xml` file is a standard XML file, somewhat similar to XHTML. The first line is a declaration for XML and the next for Voice XML. The meta maintainer tag lets the server know who's managing this application. This is useful because the Prophecy server can send detailed reports of all errors to this email address.

The `<form>` tag defines a "dialog" in voice XML. It's one interaction with the caller. In our application, we have only one interaction so far, hence only one form. Within the form we have a `<block>` of tags. Blocks are sub-divisions of a form. The `<audio>` tag is our main tag. We specified the location of the audio we want to play in the `src` attribute. The text within the `<audio>` tags is the alternative text that should be played as voice if the source file is not found. This is a good backup mechanism and should always be used.

Now that we have the welcome part done, let's figure out how we can prompt the caller to select an option and process that.

Making Choices by Key Presses

We want the caller to select if she or he wants to order a pizza online or talk to our chef. And we want her or him to do this by pressing a key. We need to recognize the key she or he pressed, and if it is a valid key, redirect control to the next form.

To take any input from the caller, we need to add a field to our VXML form.

`<field>` is very similar to an `<input>` tag in HTML. Within the `<field>` element, we can `<prompt>` the user with choices. The user will make a choice after we have completed prompting. And then, we can recognize what she or he entered.

To do any recognition—voice or keystroke—we need to develop grammar. The grammar rules will define what are valid inputs, and which field should be populated with what value when a valid input is received. Once the field is populated with the recognized value, VoiceXML can check the value of the field and decide on the next action.

With this knowledge, let us see how to put things together.

Time for Action: Prompting the User for Next Action

1. First, let us create a field in the form to accept user input. Add the following code right after the `</block>` line in our `index.xml` file.

```
<field name="option">
<grammar src="dtmf_grammar.xml" type="application/grammar-xml"/>
    <prompt>
```

```
    Press one to order a pizza online.
    Press nine to speak to our chef.
    Press zero at any time to return to this menu.
    </prompt>
</field>
```

2. The code we added will prompt the user to make a choice. We need to validate the user input via the grammar. We have already added a `<grammar>` tag to the `<field>` tag, so let us create a new file called `dtmf_grammar.xml` with the following code:

```
<?xml version="1.0" encoding="UTF-8"?>
<grammar root="MAINRULE" mode="dtmf" xmlns="http://www.
            w3.org/2001/06/grammar" xml:lang="en-US">
<rule id="MAINRULE">
<item repeat="1">
    <ruleref uri="#DTMFDIGIT"/>
    <tag>assign(digit $return)</tag>
</item>
<tag><![CDATA[ <option ($digit)> ]]> </tag>
</rule>
<rule id="DTMFDIGIT">
<one-of>
    <item> 0 <tag>return ("zero")</tag></item>
    <item> 1 <tag>return ("one")</tag></item>
    <item> 9 <tag>return ("nine")</tag></item>
</one-of>
</rule>
</grammar>
```

3. In the grammar file we defined that the value should be populated in the `option` field name using a `<tag>` element. Once the field is filled, we would like to navigate the user to another form we will create. The following code shows how we can handle this. Add this code after the `</field>` line in `index.xml`.

```
<filled>
    <if cond="option == 'one'">
        <goto next="order.xml#pizzaSelection"/>
    <elseif cond="option == 'nine'"/>
        <goto next="#callChef"/>
    <elseif cond="option == 'zero'"/>
        <goto next="#main"/>
    </if>
</filled>
```

4. We don't have a form with `id callChef`, or the `order.xml` file, but let's go ahead and run this code. It will welcome the caller, prompt her or him to make a choice, and act on the choice if valid! When you press 1 or 9, you will hear an error message because the form/file does not exists.

How Does All This Fit Together?

Let's take it bite by bite and understand how it's working.

The `<field>` tag is required to take any kind of input. The `<prompt>` tag plays back all text in it as audio. As a matter of fact, all text within tags in a VXML document will be played back as audio (almost!). We have named our field as `option`, and we will use this name later to check its value.

The grammar file is critical. The first two lines define that it's a Grammar XML file, the mode of grammar is DTMF (key presses), and that the default rule in this file is MAINRULE. The DTMFDIGIT rule dictates that it can accept any one of the digits 1, 9, and 0, and when any one of them is received, it should return an appropriate string value to the calling rule. We can use the numbers 1, 9, and 0 here because we have kept the mode of the grammar file as DTMF, else we would have to use `dtmf-1`, `dtmf-9`, and `dtmf-0`. But of course, switching the mode is what good programmers do!

The MAINRULE has a single item that has to occur once and only once. That item is the DTMFDIGIT rule. A rule can refer other rules using the `<ruleref>` tag.

Let's look at `<tag>` now. We have seen three different ways of using it in this file:

- `<tag>assign(digit $return)</tag>`
- `<tag><![CDATA[ <option ($digit)> ]]> </tag>`
- `<tag>return ("zero")</tag>`

Essentially, `<tag>` is used to define what should be done as a result of this item. In the first case, we assign the value returned from the called rule to a variable. In the second case, we assign the value of the variable to a field in the VXML file. We enclose it in CDATA as we have `<` and `>` in the value. The last case is used in rules that are called from other rules. In this case, we return the value zero. Returning values like this allows us to keep the assignment to the VXML field in a single place; and calling another rule from the main rule allows us to keep things modular and flexible.

Keep a Watch on Your Syntax

Make sure you make your VXML and grXML files in correct syntax. Wrong syntax is the cause of major development problems in voice applications. As a test, you can open the XML file with a web browser and verify that all tags are nested correctly.

If you still have problems, check the messages in the Log Viewer.

The `<filled>` code segment is executed once the grammar is processed and our `option` field is populated. Notice how the condition is written in double quotes. That's why values are enclosed in single quotes in conditions.

The `<goto>` element facilitates navigation in VoiceXML—just like the `<a>` tag in HTML. The value of the next attribute can be another form in the same document, or another VXML file. You can also point to a particular form within another VXML file, e.g. if we want to take the caller to pizza selection form with `order.xml#pizzaSelection`.

That's the first cut of our pizza ordering application. We promised the caller we will connect them to our chef if they press 9. Let's see how we can do that now!

Transferring Calls in Voice XML

When we want to connect our customers with our chef, we need to call our 1-800 number and transfer the line. VXML has a simple tag for this: `<transfer>`. You can specify the destination number and protocol in it, and the server will automatically call that number, and bridge the lines when connected.

So this could be the code to connect our caller to our chef:

```
<transfer name="chefCall" dest="tel:+18007687669" bridge="true"
connecttimeout="20s">
```

But what if the line is busy? What if someone calls at 3 A.M. and Luigi can't pick up the phone? And hey, what if someone entered 4 in our first menu? Or what if they did not understand what to do and kept holding the receiver? We need to build some error handling!

Handling Errors

Voice XML provides events for many common problems. For example to take some action when the user input did not match any rules in the grammar, we can use the `<nomatch>` tag. We can use the `<noinput>` tag and write a `<prompt>` in it, or even `<reprompt>` the last prompt if there was no input from the user. We can raise our custom events and log errors to the log file too.

These events can be handled at the document level, providing a common fallback for any problems—we will do just that!

Now that we have grasped these concepts, let us review our complete `index.xml` file.

```
<?xml version="1.0" encoding="UTF-8"?>
<vxml version = "2.1">
  <meta name="maintainer" content="youremail@yourdomain.com"/>
```

```
<link dtmf="0" next="#main"/>
<form id="main">
 <block>
   <audio src="welcome.wav">Welcome to Pizza On The Run.</audio>
 </block>
 <field name="option">
   <grammar src="dtmf_grammar.xml" type="application/grammar-xml"/>
   <prompt>Press one to order a pizza online.
   Press nine to speak to our chef.
   Press zero at any time to return to this menu.
   </prompt>
 </field>
 <filled>
   <if cond="option == 'one'">
    <goto next="order.xml#pizzaSelection"/>
   <elseif cond="option == 'nine'"/>
    <goto next="#callChef"/>
   <elseif cond="option == 'zero'"/>
    <goto next="#main"/>
   </if>
 </filled>
</form>
<form id="callChef">
 <block>
   <prompt>Please wait while I connect you to our chef
   </prompt>
   <transfer name="chefCall" dest="tel:+18007687669"
                       bridge="true" connecttimeout="20s">
    <filled>
      <if cond="chefCall == 'busy'">
       <prompt>Sorry, looks like chef is busy talking to
                                          someone else.
       </prompt>
      <elseif cond="chefCall == 'noanswer'"/>
       <prompt>Umm.. the chef is not answering. May be he is
                                          making some pizza!
       </prompt>
      <elseif cond="chefCall == 'far_end_disconnect'"/>
       <prompt>Chef hung up on you. I hope the call went well!
       </prompt>
      <elseif cond="chefCall == 'near_end_disconnect'"/>
       <prompt>Thank you for taking time to speak to our chef.
                                  I think he liked your call.
       </prompt>
      </if>
```

```
      </filled>
    </transfer>
  </block>
 </form>
 </form>
 <noinput>
  <prompt>I did not hear anything.  Please try again.</prompt>
  <reprompt/>
 </noinput>
 <nomatch>
  <prompt>Sorry, I did not understand that.</prompt>
  <reprompt/>
 </nomatch>
</vxml>
```

As we discussed, the `<noinput>` and `<nomatch>` elements are written at the document level, and repeat the last prompt after letting the user know that the system couldn't match or understand what they said/pressed.

Error handling for the `<transfer>` tag is a little different. When the transfer tag executes, the result will be populated in the `chefCall` field. The status values are self-explanatory—busy, noanswer, far_end_disconnect, and near_end_disconnect.

Adding Global Navigation with the <link> Tag

One new thing you may notice with this code is the use of a `<link>` tag near the top of the document. Here's what we have: `<link dtmf="0" next="#main"/>`. This tag takes the caller to the main form, if they press 0 from anywhere in the application.

How about ordering pizzas now? Are we ready for it yet? How will we prompt and detect which pizza the caller wants? We can give them a set of options and ask them to press a key to select one of them. But what's the fun in that? How about them saying what pizza they want and our system understanding it?

Sounds interesting? Let's figure it out!

Recognizing Voice

We know that we can do speech recognition in our voice application. We have already seen how we can prompt the user to select an option. But how do we actually do speech recognition?

We offer three pizzas on our voice application: Vegi Delight, Bacons Cheese Treat, and Pepperoni Spice. If we asked the user which pizza they want, and just caught any of the words in pizza's names, we can understand what's the match. Let's make the grammar for this.

```xml
<?xml version="1.0" encoding="UTF-8"?>
<grammar root="PIZZA" xmlns="http://www.w3.org/2001/06/grammar" xml:
lang="en-US">

<rule id="PIZZA" scope="public">
<one-of>
    <item> vegi <tag><![CDATA[ <pizza "Vegi Delight"> ]]></tag></item>
    <item> delight <tag><![CDATA[ <pizza "Vegi Delight">
                                                ]]></tag></item>
    <item> pepperoni <tag><![CDATA[ <pizza "Pepperoni Spice">
                                                ]]></tag></item>
    <item> spice <tag><![CDATA[ <pizza "Pepperoni Spice">
                                                ]]></tag></item>
    <item> bacon <tag><![CDATA[ <pizza "Bacon Cheese Treat">
                                                ]]></tag></item>
    <item> cheese <tag><![CDATA[ <pizza "Bacon Cheese Treat">
                                                ]]></tag></item>
    <item> treat <tag><![CDATA[ <pizza "Bacon Cheese Treat">
                                                ]]></tag></item>
</one-of>
</rule>
</grammar>
```

If you observe the above code, you will notice it's quite simple. We match any word from the names of the pizzas and assign the full name of the pizza to a VXML field called `pizza`. There is only one rule in the file, and it is also the root rule.

What do we do after recognizing the pizza? We need to ask the user for the crust and size she or he wants, the topping she or he would like, and then confirm the order. We will need to store all her or his selections into some variables and then pass them on to the server where we will save the order.

Storing Variables at the Application Level

Before we can pass variables to the server side, we need to create variables! VXML provides a mechanism to store variables at application level. Even if you have multiple XML files in the same application, they can access these variables from the application scope.

We can define an application-level variable at the top of the VXML document like this: `<var name="pizza" expr="''"/>`. The expression can contain a valid expression enclosed in double quotes. We want to start with a blank string, so our expression will be just two single quotes.

The actual value will be filled once we get the input from the user. We can write a tag like `<assign name="application.pizza" expr="pizza$.interpretation.pizza"/>` to assign the grammar interpretation of the pizza field to the application-level variable pizza.

`$` is a special shadow variable that stores details of the pizza interpretation. `interpretation.pizza` refers to the value assigned to pizza field from grammar. The shadow variable can also tell you the confidence in speech recognition and the way the word was uttered. But let's stay on our job for now!

Detecting the Caller's Phone Number

If we want to take an order, we need to know who ordered it! How will we do that? If we can find the caller's phone number, we can obtain the rest of the details from our existing customer database, or call her or him up and find out the address. Caller ID is very critical to any telephony provider (how will they bill them otherwise?), so we can easily get the caller's phone number.

It will be available in the `session.callerid` variable throughout our application. And as it goes, even the number they called will be available in the `session.calledid` variable!

Time for Action: Let's Put It All Together

Let's put what we have learned about application variables, caller ID, and pizza grammar in code now.

1. Create a file called `order.xml` in the same directory as `index.xml`.

2. Enter the following code in the `order.xml` file.

```
<?xml version="1.0" encoding="UTF-8"?>
<vxml version = "2.1" application="index.xml">
<meta name="maintainer" content="youremail@yourdomain.com"/>
<link dtmf="0" next="index.xml#main"/>
<!-- Variables to store order information -->
<var name="pizza" expr="''"/>
<var name="size" expr="''"/>
<var name="crust" expr="''"/>
<var name="topping" expr="''"/>
```

```
<var name="quantity" expr="''"/>
<var name="customer" expr="''"/>
<form id="pizzaSelection">
<field name="pizza">
<grammar src="pizza_grammar.xml" type="application/grammar-xml"/>
<prompt>Which Pizza do you want to order? We've got Vegi Delight,
                Pepperoni Spice and Bacon Cheese Treat.</prompt>
<noinput>
  <prompt>Sorry, I could not hear you. Please say again.</prompt>
  <reprompt/>
</noinput>
<nomatch>
  <prompt>Umm, that's not a pizza we make. Please try again.
                                        </prompt>
  <reprompt/>
</nomatch>
</field>
<filled namelist="pizza" mode="all">
<assign name="application.customer" expr="session.callerid"/>
<assign name="application.pizza" expr="pizza$.
                                    interpretation.pizza"/>
  <prompt>
   You chose <value expr="application.pizza" />.
  </prompt>
  <goto next="#crustSelection" />
</filled>
</form>
</vxml>
```

3. If you haven't already, create a `pizza_grammar.xml` file in the same folder and put in the previous code in it.

4. You can now make a call to our application again. Select 1 to order a pizza and you will be asked to select the pizza you want.

5. Say out a word that's not in our grammar file! You will get the `nomatch` message and be asked to make the selection again.

6. Say a valid name and you will get a confirmation voice letting you know the pizza you selected!

What's Cooking There?

Notice that we specified an `application` attribute in our `<vxml>` tag. This is necessary to use application-level variables. The value should be the name of the main XML file—`index.xml` in our case. Similarly, we have changed the reference in the `<link>` tag to point to the main form in `index.xml`.

Comments in VXML are within `<!--` and `-->`, just as in any other XML document. Our list of application variables is defined before our main form.

We want to customize the message given on different forms, so we have kept the `nomatch` and `noinput` tags within the form.

The `<filled>` tag has two new attributes. The `namelist` attribute specifies fields that should be populated to execute this `<filled>` code segment, the `mode` defines whether `all` of those fields should be filled or `any` before the block gets executed.

When we talked about the `$` shadow variable earlier, we did not mention that it's possible to populate multiple fields from the grammar file. Here's that trick. Something like this in our grammar file:

```
<item> something <tag><![CDATA[ <pizza "Best Pizza"> <size "Best
Size">]]></tag></item>
```

And this in our VXML:

```
<assign name="application.pizza" expr="pizza$.interpretation.
pizza"/>
<assign name="application.size" expr="pizza$.interpretation.
size"/>
```

The `pizza` and `interpretation` variables act much like an object.

`pizza` and `size` selection become properties of that object.

One more trick is to evaluate expressions as needed to get their value. In our case, we are evaluating the value of the pizza the user said and informing them in a `<prompt>`.

We have stored the caller ID in an application variable `customer`. This is not really required because we can access it from the session scope later. But we are doing this to keep things consistent, and also to allow us to extend the way we determine the customer later.

Understanding Prophecy Error Messages

If you get an MRCP error when you run your application, your grammar file has a problem. Double-check and correct it. If you get an error message that says could not connect to dialog, there is a problem in your VXML code—including linked files.

Looking Under the Hood: Which Words are Being Recognized?

In the Log Viewer, create a new filter. For the filter condition select **Message, contains** and put **Partial result** as value. When you apply this filter, you will see the results of the speech recognition engine as it does its work.

We have traveled a good distance. Congratulations!

Now, let's see how we can handle some complex grammar rules. Let's have the user say both the size and crust in the same prompt and detect what she said!

Writing Complex Grammar Rules

We want to ask the customer to speak the size of pizza and the crust she or he wants in a single input. She or he could say "twelve inch deep" or "twelve inch deep crust" or "medium and deep crust", or any other combination. We will define some intelligent rules to handle all these conditions and return the crust and the size.

Time for Action: Writing Complex Grammars

1. Create a new grammar file called `size_grammar.xml`.

2. Let's start with pieces. Let's first write the grammar rule for size. The following code shows this grammar.

    ```
    <rule id="SIZE">
    <one-of>
        <item>twelve<tag>return ("Medium")</tag></item>
        <item>medium<tag>return ("Medium")</tag></item>
        <item>fourteen<tag>return ("Large")</tag></item>
        <item>large<tag>return ("Large")</tag></item>
    </one-of>
    </rule>
    ```

3. Let us add another rule for the crusts now.

    ```
    <rule id="CRUST">
    <one-of>
        <item>deep<tag>return ("Deep")</tag></item>
        <item>thin<tag>return ("Thin")</tag></item>
    </one-of>
    </rule>
    ```

4. It's now time to write our main rule, which will call these two rules. Make sure to make it the root rule in the `<grammar>` tag.

    ```
    <rule id="SIZECRUST">
    <item>
    <item>
        <ruleref uri="#SIZE"/>
        <tag>assign(size $return)</tag>
    </item>
    <item repeat="0-1">inch</item>
    ```

```
<item repeat="0-1">and</item>
<item>
<ruleref uri="#CRUST"/>
     <tag>assign(crust $return)</tag>
</item>
<item repeat="0-1">crust</item>
</item>
<tag><![CDATA[ <crust (strcat(strcat($size '|') $crust))>
                                              ]]></tag>
</rule>
```

5. If you noticed, we have concatenated the size and crust with a pipe. That's the value our VXML crust field will receive. How do we break that apart? Here's a little secret! VXML supports JavaScript! We can write a JavaScript function to split the string at the pipe character and return the first or second part as required. Let's write up this small function in our `order.xml`, right after the application variable declarations:

```
<script>
<![CDATA[
function getValueFromPhrase(phrase, pos)
{
  phrase = phrase.toString();
  if (phrase.indexOf("|") > 0)
  {
   var valArr = phrase.split("|");
   if (valArr.length-1 > pos)
   {
      return valArr[pos];
   }
   else
   {
      return valArr[valArr.length-1];
   }
  }
  return phrase;
}
]]>
</script>
```

6. Now let's add the `crustSelection` form to our `order.xml` file. Add the following code after the `pizzaSelection` form.

```
<form id="crustSelection">
<field name="crust">
<grammar src="size_grammar.xml" type="application/grammar-xml"/>
```

```
<prompt>We make medium and large pizzas with thin crust or
                                        deep crust.
   What size and crust do you want?
</prompt>
<noinput>
  <prompt>Sorry, I could not hear you. Please say again.</prompt>
  <reprompt/>
</noinput>
<nomatch>
  <prompt>Sorry, I did not understand. Please say size followed
                              by crust choice.</prompt>
  <reprompt/>
</nomatch>
</field>
<filled namelist="crust" mode="all">
<assign name="application.size" expr="getValueFromPhrase(
                        crust$.interpretation.crust, 0)"/>
<assign name="application.crust" expr="getValueFromPhrase
                  (crust$.interpretation.crust, 1)"/>
  <prompt>Ok. <value expr="application.crust" />
                  <value expr="application.size" />.</prompt>
  <goto next="#toppingSelection" />
</filled>
</form>
```

7. That completes it. Give the app a shot and see how you get the crust and size selections.

What Just Happened? How Did it Work?

Here's some insight on what's happening!
The main grammar rule—SIZECRUST—calls in the size and crust rules. In between, it puts in items that may or may not occur in the input, like inch, and/or crust.

`strcat` is a function available in grammar XML that allows you to join two strings. Note that there is no comma between the two arguments, and the order of execution is from the innermost to the outermost.

Our JavaScript function takes a string and an index position. It converts the input parameter to a string if it is an object. Then it checks if there is a pipe character in the string. If there is, it will split the string at the pipe. It validates the `pos` argument next, returning the item at that position if valid, and the last element if invalid. If no conditions are matched, it returns the string version of the input phrase.

The VXML code is quite similar to what we have seen so far, except the assignment of value to the application variable. We call the JavaScript function with the interpretation of the crust field, and pass 0 or 1, telling the function to return the first or second value. The prompt after that confirms the values set in the application variables.

Selecting the Topping and Quantity

Selecting the topping and quantity can be done just like selecting pizzas. For toppings, we have mushroom and olive available. A simple `<one-of>` rule will suffice here. For quantities, the value can range from 1 to 9. We can recognize and handle them like this: `<item>one<tag><![CDATA[ <qty "1"> ]]></tag></item>`.

We are not going to cover toppings and quantity here to save space. But once you have added the forms and grammar for them, we can go ahead and confirm the order details with the customer, and submit the order to the server for further processing. Shall we jump on to that now?

Confirming and Submitting an Order

Once we have got all the order details, we would like to confirm them with the customer before we place the order. This is important because we want to eliminate problems of bad speech recognition. After confirmation, we would send it to our web server. The order should be saved and added to our normal order queue.

Time for Action: Confirming and Submitting an Order

1. The first thing we want to do is to repeat what options the customer has chosen, and ask her or him to confirm them. The following code shows the `confirmOrder` form that we need to add right after the quantity selection form is complete.

```
<form id="confirmOrder">
<field name="confirm" slot="confirm">
  <grammar src="confirm_grammar.xml" type="
                              application/grammar-xml"/>
  <prompt bargein="false">
   You ordered <value expr="application.quantity" /> <value
      expr="application.size" /> <value expr="application.pizza" />
      with <value expr="application.crust" /> crust and <value
      expr="application.topping" /> topping.
      Should I take the order?
```

```
        </prompt>
    </field>
    <filled namelist="confirm" mode="all">
      <if cond="confirm == 'Yes'">
         <goto next="#placeOrder" />
      <elseif cond="confirm == 'No'" />
      <prompt>Ok. Let us do it again.</prompt>
         <goto next="#pizzaSelection" />
      </if>
    </filled>
    </form>
```

2. Our confirmation grammar is simple. We check for different words the
    customer can say to confirm the order and return a Yes or a No. Here's how it
    will look:

```
<?xml version="1.0" encoding="UTF-8"?>
<grammar root="CONFIRM" xmlns="http://www.w3.org/2001/06
                              /grammar" xml:lang="en-US">
<rule id="CONFIRM">
<one-of>
    <item>yes<tag><![CDATA[ <confirm "Yes"> ]]></tag></item>
<item>yep<tag><![CDATA[ <confirm "Yes"> ]]></tag></item>
<item>yeah<tag><![CDATA[ <confirm "Yes"> ]]></tag></item>
<item>no<tag><![CDATA[ <confirm "No"> ]]></tag></item>
<item>nope<tag><![CDATA[ <confirm "No"> ]]></tag></item>
<item>nah<tag><![CDATA[ <confirm "No"> ]]></tag></item>
</one-of>
</rule>
</grammar>
```

3. Once the order is confirmed, we need to place it on the server. For this we
    need to send all application-level variables that we collected to our web
    server. As you may have guessed, this can be achieved with one tag. The
    <submit> tag. We specify the server URL in the next attribute, and the
    variables to pass in namelist. When control comes to this place, Prophecy
    will make a request to the URL, passing these variables, and play back the
    response to the caller online. The following code shows the VXML code for
    the placeOrder form.

```
<form id="placeOrder">
<block>
<submit next="http://localhost/potr/takeIVROrder.php"
              namelist="application.pizza application.size
              application.crust application.topping application.
              quantity application.customer" method="post"/>
</block>
</form>
```

4. On the server side, we need to create a new page called `takeIVROrder.php`. We can do all the business logic for handling IVR orders there. We can find a customer record from our database based on the caller ID of the person ordering, or insert a new record for that customer. If we have record for the customer in our database, we don't need to get their address; else, we need to call her or him back and take the address. The following code is a sample that simply writes out all the incoming variables to a text file. We have omitted the implementation for this example.

```php
<?php
header("Content-Type: text/xml");
echo "<?xml version=\"1.0\" encoding=\"UTF-8\"?>";
?>
<vxml version = "2.1">
<meta name="maintainer" content="youremail@yourdomain.com"/>
<?php
file_put_contents("vars.txt", print_r($_POST, true));
?>
<form id="orderPlaced">
<block>
<prompt>Order confirmed. We will call you back soon to
                       take your address. Thank you.
   </prompt>
</block>
</form>
</vxml>
```

5. Now that we have done everything, it's time to give our application a shot. Come back to the SIP phone, and dial into the application. Select your pizza, size, and crust, the topping you want, and the quantity you want to order. Listen to the confirmation; say yes, and bingo, the order is in!

How Did It Turn It All Around?

We used all the application variables we gathered in the prompt to confirm the order. If you noticed we stuck a `bargein="false"` attribute on our `<prompt>` to make sure nothing can disturb the process. Once we got the confirmation of the order, we passed a list of variables to our PHP script.

The variables will come in PHP a little differently from what we mentioned. They will become `application_pizza`, `application_size`, and so on. For now, we simply write them out to a text file to confirm the order goes through.

It's critical that our PHP outputs valid VXML code. Prophecy will not be able to play it back to the caller otherwise. Worse yet, it will play an error message to the user. To ensure success here, we put the proper XML header and prolog at the start of the PHP file. The rest of the code in PHP is standard VXML code.

> You can generate your full voice XML application using PHP. PHP can pull up information from the database, based on the user's inputs, and generate VXML or grXML content. All we need to ensure is valid VXML and grXML code so that the server can play it back as audio.

If you are waiting for more, there is none! We have achieved the titanic feat of taking a complete pizza order on the phone. Here are some online resources that will help you in developing voice applications:

- Voxeo's VXML Developers Guide: `http://www.voicexml-guide.com/`
- Ken Rehor's World of Voice XML: `http://www.kenrehor.com/voicexml/`
- Reviews, Events and more: `http://www.voicexmlplanet.com/`

What's next in VXML? `http://www.voicexml.org/`. Now, let's see what we did in this chapter!

Summary

In this chapter, we learned to develop voice-enabled dynamic applications. Specifically:

- Understanding the basics of IVR and telephony
- Setting up a Voxeo Prophecy server for development
- Creating voice applications using VXML and grXML grammar
- Playing pre-recorded audio and automatic text to speech
- Accepting keypad inputs
- Recognizing different spoken words via simple to complex grammars
- Processing data in VXML with JavaScript
- Integrating with server-side scripting and generating dynamic VXML pages

Luigi is extremely pleased now! He's got everything he wanted, but then he wants some more! Luigi's heard enough of AJAX for the web, and he is wondering if we can do AJAX on the mobile web! AJAX on the mobile web? Here comes the next chapter!

10
Mobile AJAX

AJAX and Web 2.0 are two expressions that web developers have uttered a million times in the last two years. Apart from being hot buzzwords, they actually represent advances in technology that facilitate building better web applications. AJAX is now possible even on mobile devices, and Luigi is interested in exploring what can be done for Pizza On The Run.

In this chapter, we will learn how to use AJAX on mobile devices. We will specifically look at:

- Getting pizza recipes via AJAX
- Enabling AJAX in forms
- Understanding iPhone application development
- More of building rich mobile apps

Mobile devices have limited CPU power, memory, and network speed. These restrict the usage of scripting in the browser. Most of the time, it's not feasible to allow scripting. Loops in JavaScript and XML DOM (Document Object Model) processing can also drain the batteries as they involve a lot of CPU cycles. A mobile device can be on the move, so the network connection may drop and reconnect and is not very reliable.

But with better phones, it is now possible to run JavaScript-based AJAX applications on mobile devices. On the extreme side, AJAX applications are the only way to build and run custom applications on a device like the iPhone.

Let's now see how we can use these technologies!

Getting Pizza Recipes via AJAX

Luigi wants to build a social tool where visitors can participate. He wants to share pizza recipes, and even allow visitors to contribute their own recipes. But more importantly, he wants to allow them to comment on a recipe, share their experiences cooking that recipe, and get connected with other pizza lovers!

The following figure shows how the page will be laid out for the new Recipes section on Pizza On The Run. The recipe and comments are the main sections of the page. Navigation at the top will allow visitors to traverse between recipes.

Devising our AJAX Strategy

We are assuming that you have a fair understanding of the basic AJAX concepts. If you are new to AJAX, it's a good time to read Jesse James Garrett's article at http://www.adaptivepath.com/publications/essays/archives/000385.php that started the whole AJAX revolution. Googling for AJAX too will give you a wealth of information on the topic.

If you think about it, the main advantage of AJAX is reduced page reloads. We can retrieve only the data that we want from the server, and change only the part of the page that we want to change. This makes the interface more interactive and fluid. For our recipes page, we want to bring the recipe and comments via AJAX. The comment submission too will happen over AJAX.

But hey, AJAX has XML in it! Are we really going to use XML? If we use XML, the mobile browser has to process the XML, format it, and then display it. This could take up a lot of CPU power. So what can we do? Simple; don't use XML! Use XHTML! We will format the output on the server, and the client will only have to display that at an appropriate place in the page. This will make our job easier. So as such, we will be using AJAH (Asynchronous JavaScript and HTML) and not AJAX! Another caveat is the use of JavaScript! The purpose of mobile AJAX is to make things faster. So, we need to ensure that our JavaScript neither takes too long to download, nor takes the CPU for a spin!

If you have worked with AJAX on the Web, you will be aware of many libraries and tools available to build AJAX applications. Dojo, Prototype, YUI, and Script.actulo. us are some of the most popular toolkits. Unfortunately, there are no such libraries available for mobile AJAX as of this writing. There are a few projects under way, but none released to the public. A mobile AJAX library must be lightweight and ideally, be adapted as per the device—exposing features supported only by that device. If we don't want to get into a lot of complexity, implementing basic AJAX is very simple. We can use the `XMLHttpRequest` object to build our AJAX application.

What we will do is extend the Frost AJAX library. Frost is the first mobile AJAX library, and is still under development. Available from Paving Ways (`www.pavingways.com`), Frost provides the basic AJAX functions. We will write additional JavaScript code to serve our needs and glue things together.

On the back end, we will write code that will retrieve the recipe and comment information. One important thing we need to keep in mind here is that only the recipe and comments HTML code should be outputted. No `<body>` or other XHTML tags are necessary. This is because whatever our back end will output will come to the AJAX call. And that is what will be inserted into the `<div>` that shows recipes and comments. If we have extra HTML code, that too will be inserted in the `<div>`, making our document syntactically incorrect. It may also affect the way the page is displayed.

We have a problem to solve here. All our back end gets routed through `index.php`, hence the header and other files get included automatically on all calls. We do not need them on our AJAX calls. To avoid this, we will use PHP's output buffering system. In `index.php`, we will start buffering the output via `ob_start()`. At the end of `index.php`—once all operations are done—we will flush the output buffer with `ob_end_flush()`. This will ensure other pages work well. Now at the beginning of our AJAX handler, we will simply do an `ob_end_clean()` to discard current output buffers and stop further buffering. We can then output whatever we want. At the end of our handler, we will `exit()`, so that no footer code will be shown as well.

In terms of page structure, we will have a few `<div>` tags. The main div will be the one that will hold the recipe and comments. We will have a div for the comment form also—but it will be hidden at the start. We will have a `<script>` area where we will keep all our functions that use the Frost library and perform operations that we want.

We now have the fundamentals in place. Let's go ahead and implement the recipes page!

Time for Action: Showing Recipes

1. We need to first create two tables—one for recipes and the other for comments. The following code shows the SQL to create these tables.

    ```
    CREATE TABLE `recipes` (
        `id` int(10) unsigned NOT NULL auto_increment,
        `submitter` varchar(75) NOT NULL,
        `submitterPhone` varchar(20) NOT NULL,
        `photo` varchar(30) NOT NULL,
        `dateUpdated` timestamp NOT NULL,
        `title` varchar(30) NOT NULL,
        `basicInfo` mediumtext NOT NULL,
        `ingredients` mediumtext NOT NULL,
        `directions` mediumtext NOT NULL,
        PRIMARY KEY  (`id`)
    ) COMMENT='Hot recipes';
    CREATE TABLE `recipeComments` (
        `id` int(10) unsigned NOT NULL auto_increment,
        `recipeId` int(11) unsigned NOT NULL,
        `submitter` varchar(75) NOT NULL,
        `submitterPhone` varchar(20) NOT NULL,
        `dateUpdated` timestamp NOT NULL,
        `comment` mediumtext NOT NULL,
        PRIMARY KEY  (`id`)
    ) COMMENT='Comments on recipes';
    ```

2. We can now add a few recipes and comments via phpMyAdmin, so that when we do the rest of the code, we have some data to display. While adding data, please ensure that you use proper `recipeId` values in the `recipeComments` table.

3. Let us create the Recipe class now. It will extend the BaseModel class we have been using in the rest of the POTR code, and will make it easy to retrieve or save data from the recipe table. The following code shows this class.

    ```php
    <?php
    class Recipe extends BaseModel
    {
        public $_submitter;
        public $_submitterPhone;
    ```

```php
    public $_photo;
    public $_dateUpdated;
    public $_basicInfo;
    public $_ingredients;
    public $_directions;
    public function __construct($tableName = "recipes",
                                        $data = null)
    {
        parent::__construct($tableName, $data);
    }
}
?>
```

4. Similarly, we can create the RecipeComment class. Let's add a function to get all comments for a particular recipe too.

```php
<?php
class RecipeComment extends BaseModel
{
    public $_recipeId;
    public $_dateUpdated;
    public $_submitter;
    public $_submitterPhone;
    public $_comment;
    public function __construct($tableName = "recipeComments",
                                        $data = null)
    {
        parent::__construct($tableName, $data);
    }
    public function GetCommentsForRecipe($recipeId)
    {
        return $this->GetAll("recipeId = '$recipeId'",
                                    "dateUpdated desc");
    }
}
?>
```

5. It's time to create a PHP file that will show the recipes to the visitor. This file will also make the AJAX calls and provide a form to comment on a recipe. First, let's get the structure ready. Refer to the following code for `recipes.inc.php`'s first cut!

```html
<div id="jsarea">
<script type="text/javascript" src="assets/frost.js"></script>
<script type="text/javascript">
<![CDATA[
// Check for AJAX support. If not supported, show a warning
if (!TestXHR())
```

```
{
    document.write("Your browser has JavaScript support, but no
                                        AJAX support.");
}
else
{
    // Get a recipe via AJAX
}
]]>
</script>
<noscript>Sorry your browser does not support
                            JavaScript!</noscript>
</div>
<div id="main">
    <h2>Hot Recipes</h2>
    <p>Latest recipes from POTR and our visitors!</p>
</div>
<div id="commentForm"></div>
```

6. You may have noticed the frost.js there and the call to the TestXHR()
    function. This is the Frost mobile AJAX library we talked about. The
    TestXHR() function checks if the browser has AJAX support. If the browser
    does not have AJAX or JavaScript support, we show an appropriate message.
    Ideally, we should provide such browsers with another page from which
    they can see recipes in a non-AJAX way. A nice article on dev.mobi explains
    how to do this (http://dev.mobi/node/557). We will just focus on the
    AJAX way in our examples. So let's see what's in the frost.js file.

```
var xhr = false;
var dgbcnt = 0;
// preload loading image
loading = new Image();
loading.src = "assets/loading.gif";
function dbg(message){
    dgbcnt ++;
    var messobj = document.getElementById('debug');
    if(messobj) messobj.innerHTML += dgbcnt+': '+message+'<br />';
}
function TestXHR(){
    // check for XHR support
    var xhrsupport = XHRInit();
    if(xhrsupport){
        return true;
    }
    return false;
```

```
  }
  function XHRInit() {
     if(xhr){ return "true 1"; }
     else {
        req = false;
        if(window.XMLHttpRequest) {
           try { xhr = new XMLHttpRequest(); return
                                  "XMLHttpRequest Object"; }
           catch(e) { xhr = false; return false; }
           return false;
        } else if(window.ActiveXObject) {
           try { xhr = new ActiveXObject('Msxml2.XMLHTTP');
                                  return "ActiveX"; }
           catch(e) {
              try {xhr = new ActiveXObject('Microsoft.XMLHTTP');
                       return "ActiveX";} catch(e) { xhr = false;
                                          return false; }
           }
           return false;
        } else { xhr = false; return false; }
     }
  }
  function XHRReq(url, responsediv, addcontent, returnvalue){
     if(XHRInit()){
        xhr.open('POST', url, true);
        xhr.setRequestHeader('Content-Type', 'text/html;
                                  charset=utf-8');
        xhr.onreadystatechange = function(){ if(xhr.readyState
           == 4){ ProcessXHR(xhr, responsediv, addcontent); } }
        xhr.send('');
     }
     return returnvalue;
  }
  function ProcessXHR(xmlHttpReq, responsediv, addcontent){
     var responseText = xmlHttpReq.responseText ? xmlHttpReq.
                                  responseText : '';
     if(addcontent){document.getElementById(responsediv).innerHTML
                                  += responseText;}
     else {document.getElementById(responsediv).innerHTML =
                                  responseText;}
        }
  function ShowDetails(url, responsearea, addcontent, returnvalue){
     document.getElementById(responsearea).innerHTML = '<img
              class="loadimg" src="'+loading.src+'" alt="loading..."
                                  width="16" height="16" />';
     return XHRReq(url, responsearea, addcontent, returnvalue);
}
```

7. The library now gives us functions that we can use to implement AJAX. XMLHttpRequest and response handling are essential parts of AJAX. But we still have to write our back end and extra JavaScript functions that will glue things together. Let us first build a PHP back end that will give us recipe details and comments on them. Below is the code in `recipeHandler.inc.php`—the file that will be invoked via `index.php` through AJAX.

```php
<?php
ob_end_clean();
if (!$_REQUEST['what'] || $_REQUEST['what'] == 'show')
{
    // Replace new lines with list item tags so that we can show
    //          a nice display
    function splitToList($string)
    {
        return '<li>'.str_replace("\n", "</li><li>",
                                    trim($string)).'</li>';
    }
    if(!isset($_REQUEST['num']))
    {
        $_REQUEST['num'] = 0;
    }
    $recipe = new Recipe();
    // Get recipe details - limit at num - this will
    //                                  fetch only one recipe
    $result = $recipe->GetAll("", "id desc", "1",
                                    $_REQUEST['num']);
    if (count($result) == 1)
    {
        foreach($result as $item)
        {
            echo '<h2>'.$item['title'].'</h2>
            <img src="assets/recipes/'.$item['photo'].'" alt="'
                            .$item['title'].'" /><br />
            <h3>Basic Information</h3><ul>'.splitToList(
                            $item['basicInfo']).'</ul>
<h3>Ingredients</h3><ul>'.splitToList($item['ingredients']).'</ul>
<h3>Directions</h3><ol>'.splitToList($item['directions']).'</ol>
            <p>Submitted by '.$item['submitter'].' on '.$item[
                            'dateUpdated'].'</p>';
            // Pass a hidden field. This will be required while adding
            //                                  comments later on
            echo '<form name="recipeHiddenInfo"><input type="hidden"
                    name="recipeId" value="'.$item['id'].'" /></form>';
```

```
                // Get the comments for this item
                $rc = new RecipeComment();
                $comments = $rc->GetCommentsForRecipe($item['id']);
                if (count($comments) > 0)
                {
                    echo '<h3>Comments:</h3>';
                    foreach($comments as $comment)
                    {
                        echo '<p>'.$comment['comment'].'<br />
                        By: '.$comment['submitter'].' On: '.$comment[
                                            'dateUpdated'].'</p>';
                    }
                }

            }
        }
        else
        {
            echo '<p>Sorry, no more recipes found.</p>';
        }
    }
    else if ($_REQUEST['what'] == 'comment')
    {
        // Comment saving code here
    }
    exit;
    ?>
```

8. That was a lot of PHP code! We are now ready to add JavaScript functions and get recipes! Let's give it a shot. Let's add some code to our `recipe.inc.php` in the JavaScript section. We will get a recipe if our AJAX test succeeds. Below is this code. The code to make the AJAX call is highlighted.

```
<div id="jsarea">
<script type="text/javascript" src="assets/frost.js"></script>
<script type="text/javascript">
<![CDATA[
var num = 0;
var reqNum = 0;

function GetRecipe(index)
{
    reqNum = index;
    if (reqNum >= 0)
    {
```

```
        ShowDetails('?action=recipeHandler&what=show&num='+
                        (reqNum), 'main', false, false);
    }
}
if (!TestXHR())
{
    document.write("Your browser has JavaScript support, but no
                                    AJAX support.");
}
else
{
    GetRecipe(0);
}
]]>
</script>
<noscript>Sorry your browser does not support
                                JavaScript!</noscript>
</div>
```

9. If all went well, you should see something like the following figure in your mobile browser!

10. If you face any problem, add an `alert(responseText);` after the first line in the `ProcessXHR` function in `frost.js`. That will show you the HTML code coming from the server. You may also use the `dbg()` function for any other debugging needs. If your mobile device does not support JavaScript, the following figure is what you may see.

What's Going on in the Background?

We created a platform for building AJAX-enabled applications. The way it works is that when the page gets loaded in the browser, the JavaScript will execute and check if the browser has `XMLHttpRequest` (XHR) object support. If it does, we call the `GetRecipes` function with 0 as argument. That in turn calls the `ShowDetails` function of Frost library. This put up a loading image in the main div and makes an XHR request through the `XHReq` function. This is an asynchronous call, and the `ProcessXHR` function will be called once the server's response is received.

On the server, the PHP code makes a query, and limits it for one record starting from 0. Once we get the recipe data, we format it using some nice HTML. We also use a custom function to split the data at new line characters and show it in a list format. We are using a form and a hidden variable that stores the `recipeId` in the output. This will be used later in the JavaScript function that submits a comment on a recipe. Once this is done, we check the `recipeComments` table for comments made on this `recipeId`. If we find any, we include them also in the output.

All this output from PHP comes in `ProcessXHR` as `responseText`. And we put that in the `main` div. As we do this, the page content changes and shows us our recipe! And all this happened without reloading the page!

What if Your Device Does Not Support AJAX?

If the devices you are testing on do not support AJAX, it would be difficult to test. One option is to use a service like DeviceAnywhere (www.deviceanywhere.com) that allows you to remotely test on a variety of mobile devices and carriers. You get to test on the actual devices remotely, and it's very convenient to test multiple real devices from a single place. The following screenshot shows our POTR application running in an iPhone over DeviceAnywhere.

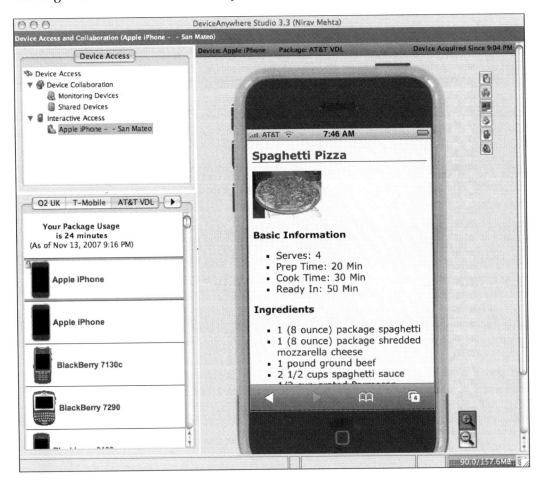

If you do not want to use DeviceAnywhere, you can test with desktop versions of Opera and Safari browsers. Many mobile browsers these days are based on the WebKit engine (http://webkit.org/) and you can test on that too. But do remember that testing on real devices may have varying results.

On the other side, what if your target users don't have AJAX support? It's always a good practice to have a backup! Though AJAX support is increasing, do take some time to build a fallback for your production applications. The dev.mobi article mentioned earlier shows a good example of how you can do this.

 While doing AJAX, don't go overboard. Animated "loading" images, animations, and other eye candy may actually hinder the usability of your application because of the download size and CPU needs. Stay focused on the user!

Adding Navigation

We got one recipe on the page. But we need a simple way to navigate within the recipes. This is very easy now with our `GetRecipe` function. What we need to keep track of is the current index of the recipe. And we can add one or subtract one from it to get the next or previous recipe. Let's code it up!

Time for Action: Adding Navigation for Recipes

1. If you noticed, in the previous code, we have checked if the requested index is greater than zero. If it is, only then we make the request to get the recipe. At the start of our JavaScript, we have initialized two variables—`num` and `reqNum`. Variable `num` will store the index of the current recipe and `reqNum` is the index of the requested recipe.

2. What remains is to set the `num` to `reqNum` once the requested recipe is received! Let us write a function that does this in `recipe.inc.php`. We will then call this function once we get the XHR response. Below is the code.

```
function ResultProcessed()
{
    num = reqNum;
}
```

3. Next, let us modify `frost.js ProcessXHR()` to call our function once the response is processed. This means once the recipe is displayed, `ResultProcessed()` will be called. If you are going to use `frost.js` in other pages, you should make sure that you have a function named `ResultProcessed()` on the page, otherwise it will throw up a JavaScript error.

```
function ProcessXHR(xmlHttpReq, responsediv, addcontent){
    var responseText = xmlHttpReq.responseText ?
                            xmlHttpReq.responseText : '';
    if(addcontent){document.getElementById(responsediv)
                            .innerHTML += responseText;}
```

```
            else {document.getElementById(responsediv).innerHTML
                                                        = responseText;}

    ResultProcessed();
}
```

4. What remains now is to link up the next and previous recipes via JavaScript. Let's add this at the top of our `recipes.inc.php`. Below is the code.

```
<p><a href="#" onclick="JavaScript:GetRecipe(num-1);">Prev recipe</a>
- <a href="#" onclick="JavaScript:GetRecipe(num+1);">Next recipe</a>
- <a href="#commentForm" onclick="JavaScript:ShowCommentForm();
">Add a Comment</a></p>
```

5. That's all! Clicking on Next or Prev on our recipes page will load up the appropriate recipe. When all recipes are finished, we will get an apology message saying there are no more recipes! The following screenshot shows what the navigation looks like, on the iPhone.

Yes! Simply setting a variable to hold the current index and adjusting it on fetching the next or previous recipe does the trick for us. The PHP back end expects just the index, and it fetches one recipe from there. When the code is done, it feels so fluid navigating among recipes! That's the power of AJAX!

Adding Comments

We want to allow users to submit comments on the recipes displayed. This will build a community around our recipes service. We have already added a link for submitting comments. Let's see how we can develop the code for it.

Time for Action: Submitting Comments

1. Let us add the comment form to `recipe.inc.php` first. We will keep it in a `<div>` and hide it by default. This will save some screen space. Below is the form code.

```
<div id="commentForm" style="display:none">
<a id="commentForm"></a>
<h2>Add a Comment</h2>
<form name="formComment">
<fieldset>
<input type="hidden" name="recipeId" value="0" />
Your Name: <input type="text" name="submitter" value=""
                              size="20" maxlength="35" /><br/>
Your Phone: <input type="text" name="submitterPhone" value=""
                              size="20" maxlength="35" /><br/>
Comment: <textarea name="comment" value="" cols="35"
                                    rows="10" ></textarea><br/>
<input type="button" value="Contribute" onClick="
                                      SubmitComment()"/>
</fieldset>
</form>
</div>
```

2. In the link we added, we have set the href to `#commentForm`, which is the anchor ID. The page will scroll to the form when the link is clicked. Let us write a function that will show the form if it's hidden, and hide it if it's visible.

```
function ShowCommentForm()
{
   var elm = document.getElementById("commentForm").style;
   if (elm.display == "none")
   {
      elm.display = "block";
   }
   else
   {
      elm.display = "none";
   }
}
```

3. When the user clicks the link, she or he will see the form. On clicking the button in the form, we are calling a JavaScript function `SubmitComment()`. What we need to do in this function is get the `recipeId` from the hidden form that the AJAX call has sent, collect other variables from the comment form, and send them to the `recipeHandler`.

```
function SubmitComment(frm)
{
    // Copy the recipeId value from the hidden form
    //                                     received from AJAX
    // to the comment form
    var src = document.recipeHiddenInfo;
    var target = document.formComment;
    var url = "?action=recipeHandler&what=comment";
    url += "&recipeId=" + src.recipeId.value;
    url += "&submitter=" + target.submitter.value;
    url += "&submitterPhone=" + target.submitterPhone.value;
    url += "&comment=" + target.comment.value;
    ShowDetails(url, 'commentForm', false, false);
}
```

4. Now we can write the back end code to save the comment to the table. It's straightforward now that we have created the `RecipeComment` class. We need to add code to the `recipeHandler` to save the comment when the value of the `what` variable is `comment`! We can populate the class with the data coming in the request, set the date, and save it. Below is the code.

```
else if ($_REQUEST['what'] == 'comment')
{
    $rc = new RecipeComment("recipeComments", $_REQUEST);
    $rc->dateUpdated = date("Y-m-d H:i:s");
    if ($rc->Save())
    {
        echo "<p>Comment saved.</p>";
    }
    else
    {
        echo "<p>Could not save your comment.</p>";
    }
}
```

5. The following screenshot shows how submitted comments and our form may display in a mobile browser. It's actually just like any other browser! And if we want to make it a bit more interesting, we can send back the actual comment in the output along with the message that the comment was saved. This will display the comment to the user, giving her or him instant gratification! That's what we want, isn't it?

What's the Deal with All that Form Code?

The biggest piece in the comments code is the form processing. It's the JavaScript way of accessing values from form elements. The source and target bit are simply pointers to two forms. The source form is the one we got from the `GetRecipe()` request, and the target form is the one the user filled. We pick up the `recipeId` from the source form (as without that, our comment will be orphaned), club it with other values from the target form, and push the URL across. We are using the POST method to send variable values via AJAX, but it is also possible to use GET.

Alright, so we have our AJAX-driven Hot Recipes section up on POTR. We have added another form for visitors to submit their own recipes, and also a comment approval system—of course we don't want spam bots to flood our recipe pages with advertisements to increase the strength/size of particular body parts! We have also created fallback systems for people who do not have AJAX devices.

So let's think about what else is possible with AJAX on the mobile.

I Want More AJAX on My Mobile!

You can do wonders with AJAX. Just like how people have built breakthrough web applications using AJAX, you can build a breakthrough mobile application using AJAX. Or if you already have a great web app, you can port it to mobile using AJAX. You can use effects and animation, drag and drop, and many other things. Just keep in mind the battery and network power your application will consume.

And if you have been looking around, you certainly want to deploy your application on the iPhone! Apple's unique mobile phone cum iPod cum dual finger scrolling machine. There are hundreds of applications already ported to iPhone—and remember, iPhone only supports browser-based applications—and many other developers are working on bringing out iPhone versions of their app.

Let's quickly look at what it takes to develop for the iPhone then!

Understanding iPhone Application Development

There are quite a few distinct features of iPhone that make it an interesting target for developing your AJAX applications. First, it's operated by a touch screen. Second, it's possible to use two fingers at once! There are interesting scroll functions on flicking your finger down the screen. To top it all, it includes an almost full-fledged Safari browser, complete with scaling and zooming to fit any website onto the iPhone.

Apple provides a comprehensive guide for developers building applications for iPhone. You can access the online documentation from `http://developer.apple.com/iphone/`. You will have to register for a free online Apple Developer Connection membership to access the documentation though.

Here are a few important points to keep in mind:

- Make sure your content and application are standards compliant—XHTML, CSS etc. If they are not, they may not display correctly.

- Keep in mind the way users will interact with their fingers. As there is no mouse, you don't have precision over where the user will tap. Keep large buttons; don't keep too many links together, and ensure that you handle only events that you want to.

- The phone can rotate and Safari will auto-rotate the application. Make sure it works well with that. You can also listen for rotation change events and redraw the page if you wish.

- The default size of the available screen for the app is 320x396 pixels. But develop for 480 pixels width; iPhone will scale it down.

- Also note that testing in Safari on the desktop and testing on iPhone are different. Don't assume something that works on Safari will work on the iPhone.

- There are no scrollbars and no windows. Whatever is the content size, iPhone will fit it into its screen size by default.

- The iPhone does not support Flash/Java/File Upload/Download. So don't use them!

- The iPhone has an onscreen keyboard. When the onscreen keyboard comes up, the space available for your application will be less. Keep your input fields limited, and together, so it's easier for the user to handle the keyboard.

- You can use iPhoney (`http://sourceforge.net/projects/iphonesimulator/`) to get an iPhone-like browser on your desktop to test your applications.

- Use iPhone features! Use an iPhone-like UI if you can! Joe Hewitt's iUI (`http://code.google.com/p/iui/`) is a great library to build iPhone-like interfaces with AJAX. The following screenshot shows a possible root-level menu for POTR using iUI, running in iPhoney shell, rotated horizontally.

- If you rely heavily on browser/mouse/key events in your application, be prepared for a lot of surprises. iPhone does not consistently emit events. You will have to figure out what works in your case and what does not.

- You can use a toolkit like Dojo (`http://www.dojotoolkit.org/`) for AJAX functions and effects. Many of the functionalities work out of the box, and the developers are working hard to make the rest work.

- People have developed many tools to hack into iPhone. Try them out. They will give you great understanding of how it works!

- And yes, read the Apple documentation on iPhone development. This will give you a kickstart. You can also go `http://www.apple.com/webapps/` and check out all the cool applications people have built so far. Go ahead, view the source and learn from it!

If all this hasn't whet your appetite for iPhone application development. The iPhone is a new genre of mobile device and a lot of future devices are going to be similar. Building for the iPhone will prepare you to deal with those new devices.

If you find the AJAX way still too restrictive, you don't have any other options with iPhone. But hey, iPhone is not the only device in the market. Not even the market leader! There are so many other mobile devices that allow you to build rich mobile applications using different technologies. Let's understand what these options are!

More Ways to Build Rich Mobile Apps

If you want to take advantage of the mobile device's operating system, you can create applications using that device's Software Development Kit. Most platforms allow you to use C or Java to create applications. If you want to deploy on a Windows mobile, you can even use .NET languages. You can write business applications, tools that take advantage of the devices' features—including accessing messages, accessories, and files on the device. You can even develop games! Such applications typically need to be downloaded and installed on the device before they can be used.

If you don't want to go too deep in C/Java/.NET, you can use Flash Lite to deploy your application. You can build the UI in Flash, and use Flash ActionScript to communicate to a server for retrieving data. Flash Lite also exposes some device functionalities that you can use.

What's more important for building mobile applications is the focus on the user's context. The technology choices will be easier once you clearly know who the target user is and how she or he is going to use your application.

Let's come back to the Mobile Web! We even learned many things about mobile AJAX development in this chapter. Let's revise what we saw.

Summary

In this chapter, we learned to AJAX-enable our applications. Specifically:

- Understanding why AJAX is relevant for mobile devices
- Building an AJAX strategy for our application
- Using HTML instead of XML to reduce client load
- Using JavaScript and PHP to dynamically fetch recipes
- Sending and retrieving data using AJAX
- Understanding iPhone app development—tips and tools

We have learned a great deal about building mobile web applications so far. We have also integrated messaging and voice support in our application. You are already a master at building mobile web applications! So what's next for us? What's next for us is what's next for everyone! Let's look at some trends and tools that promise to shape the next few years of the mobile web in the next chapter!

11
Mobile Web 3.0?

It's a Tuesday evening. Luigi Mobeeli—owner of Pizza On The Run—is sitting quietly in his balcony. Observing the evening city traffic, Luigi is a satisfied man. What was a Mom-n-Pop corner shop for decades, has now transformed into a hot favorite of geeks. Hundreds of orders come in through the mobile web, SMS, and the IVR system. Luigi's children have taken up managing most of the business in their vacation now, and the POTR team is all charged up.

A smile lights up Luigi's face as he thinks about what technology has done for him in the last three months. From a simple catalog website, Pizza On The Run has gone to mobile, then to SMS/MMS, and then to voice. The launch of the Hot Recipes section was noticed not only by customers, but even by tech journals as a cool technology implementation. Luigi was enthusiastic about technology, but never thought he would come this far. He feels proud of his technical team! "Maybe I should sponsor them a year's pizzas", he grinned.

Suddenly, the visionary businessman in Luigi wakes up! "We have done so well so far, but what about the future? What is the future of the mobile web? What are the latest trends and what can we expect to come up in the next few months?" Maybe it's time to review the current trends and start thinking about future strategy. Time to call in the experts!

Wednesday morning, Luigi calls us and shares his ideas. We know the target and are excited to do the research. Let us look at following in this chapter:

- Trends in mobile web applications
- Mobile widgets and developments of the browser
- Connectivity—mobile networks, occasionally connected devices
- Open Handset Alliance and Google's Android system
- Resources to keep abreast of the mobile scene

After we review these, we will list resources—websites, blogs, and mailing lists to visit to stay up to date on the mobile web scene. Now, let's begin by looking at the trends in mobile web applications!

Mobile Web Applications are Growing Faster than Humans

Every major web application is being ported to mobile devices. Mobile-specific new applications are being launched every day. The following screenshot shows listing of Remember The Milk (www.rememberthemilk.com) on Apple's Webapps gallery—a directory of web applications that run on the iPhone and iPod Touch, and the screenshot after that shows Yahoo!'s mobile offerings.

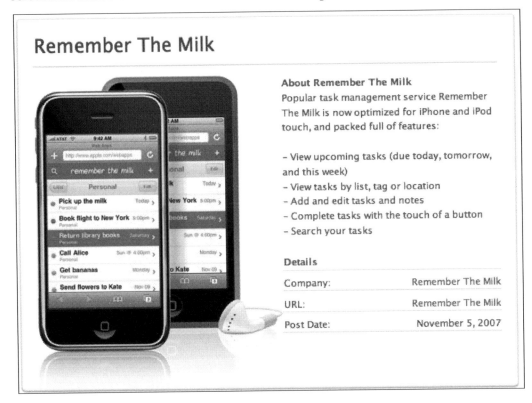

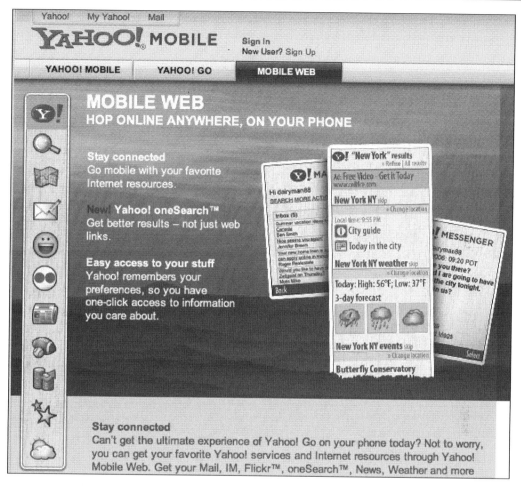

There are browser-based applications on the mobile to access email, RSS feeds, and podcasts. You can keep track of your contacts and calendars from your mobile browser. If you get bored, you can even play games! The number of native mobile applications is high, but a lot more web applications are now coming to the mobile. With more and more mobile browsers supporting XHTML, CSS, and AJAX, the job of developers to port a web application to mobile devices has become easier. We have learned the tricks of this trade throughout the book, and you too can build compelling mobile web applications.

If you see the overall picture, trends are clear:

- Port already popular web applications to mobile devices
- Provide local content, make sure to take care of context
- Use AJAX, XHTML, and CSS to deliver powerful applications

- Use SMS to supplement your mobile web offering
- Adapt design and content according to the device capabilities
- Make it simple and take everything to mobile!

Apart from that, the Web 2.0 (and 3.0) philosophies are extended to mobile. The long tail, web as a platform, user contributed content, importance of data, lightweight development, perpetual beta, rich user interface, and software as service have come to mobile now. Mashups and community are happening. We may goof up in the terminology, but the core principles of Web 2.0 are very much relevant to the mobile web.

And it is not just the browser that people are using to deliver mobile web applications! Mobile widgets are showing up as a powerful way to bring the Web to mobile devices.

Mobile Widgets and Mobile Browsers

Mobile widgets are single purpose applications. They do a particular task, are normally based on web technologies, and can access device-specific features like camera and phonebook. There are a few mobile widget platforms already, and more are coming! There is little standardization between different platforms, but things will settle in the near future. Opera is the major player for web widgets and Opera 9 has support for mobile widgets. Openwave also has a Mobile AJAX SDK that allows building widgets. Apart from these, there are players who have built their own platforms. WidSets (`www.widsets.com`) and Plusmo (`www.plusmo.com`) are popular among such platforms. There are thousands of widgets available even today! The following screenshot shows a list of featured widgets on WidSets from the 3000+ that are available.

Most platforms come with a good amount of documentation to get you started in developing your own widgets. Opera has a collection of articles at `http://dev.opera.com/articles/widgets/` explaining widgets and how to develop them.

The Advantages of Mobile Widgets

The advantages widgets have are many-fold. First, they run just like other applications on the device, not as something that needs a browser to launch. It's much easier for the user to understand and interact with widgets. A widget can access device resources that a web application cannot. A widget may even cache some data, reducing the need for AJAX calls to retrieve data. Widgets can have fancy user interfaces and cool animations. If this was not enough, the development technology is the same—XHTML, CSS, and AJAX!

Imagine a currency conversion calculator. If you build a web application for it, the user must be online to use it. But if it's a widget, once installed, it can be called up even when the user is not connected to the Web. The widget can use cached data and covert currencies on its own now.

While there are alternatives to run applications outside the browser, the browsers themselves are getting intelligent. Let's see what we can expect in the future mobile browsers.

Mobile Browsers Get Better

Today's latest mobile browsers are not much behind their desktop counterparts. They can show standard web pages in a scaled down fashion, allow the user to zoom in and pan, automatically change display if you rotate your device, support CSS and AJAX, and can do an excellent job at showing you the Internet.

But it's still difficult to use a mobile browser. Even though some browsers support opening multiple pages at once, it's difficult to navigate among them. The browser can drain the battery, run too slow, and simply can't do what a native application can do.

There are demands that browsers open up access to device capabilities to web applications, and that they execute JavaScript without burning the battery. Mobile browsers will get there. And that too quite soon!

Minimo is a mobile-specific browser from Firefox. Apple's iPhone uses Safari as its browser. Opera's browsers are getting better everyday. And many manufacturers are basing their browser implementations on WebKit (`www.webkit.org`)—making way for a standard and powerful platform to serve the Internet to the user.

Do We Need Server-Side Adaptation?

If browsers are getting standardized, do we still need server-side adaptation? The answer is: Yes! Even after standard compliance of browsers, we still have variations in screen sizes, input methods, and network speeds to deal with. These can't be dealt without adaptation at server level. Apart from the initiatives we have already talked about in the book—like WURFL and CSS—there are other interesting approaches coming up.

One such approach is W3C's DIAL—Device Independent Authoring Language. DIAL (`http://www.w3.org/TR/dial/`) is a combination of XHTML 2, XForms, and DISelect. The intention behind DIAL is to develop a language that will allow consistent delivery across devices and contexts. The DIAL processor can be on the server, at an intermediary, or on the client side. The language looks promising and flexible. So keep track of it!

On the other hand, adaptation tools are getting better and "automatic adaptation" may solve/resolve many of the issues. With increasing knowledge about the device and standards compliance, an adaptation engine should be able to take care of most of the customizations on its own—leaving the author to define rules for content adaptation.

Many mobile devices now support multiple networks. For example, the iPhone works over WiFi and EDGE. And it's almost transparent to the user. But imagine you are viewing a streaming YouTube video over WiFi and then go out of it. Switching to EDGE may happen automatically, but the video may crawl and stutter. How do you handle that?

Connectivity—Mobile Networks and Occasionally Connected Devices

If the device supports multiple wireless networks—Bluetooth, WiFi, WiMAX, EDGE, 3G, GSM, CDMA, etc.—the operating system will handle connections and disconnections. We can't handle them. The only thing we can do is to try to check the connection speed/IP address on each request and adapt content if required.

Devices that support multiple networks are a good thing for users. Some devices make a transition from one available network to another automatically. Some others require manual selection. All these complications can affect the application in use at that time. Consider that the user has selected all the pizzas and side dishes she or he wants to order, and even entered her or his address. In the final order processing step, the network changes. If we had code that will accept requests only from the previous IP address, the user will have to start the whole process again. And if the user moved from a fast network to a slow one, and we showed large size images on the order confirmation, it will be a pain for the user to wait for things to load.

As developers, we will have to learn and balance these things. User experience matters and we have got to do everything to make it easier. Remember that many mobile users will be non-geek. Most non-tech too! What matters to them is simply to get the job done.

OK, you can handle network changes and make it easier for the users. But what if the connection drops? We have been to places where even the phone network is not available — the signal strength indicator showing zero bars instead of the full five. What can we do in such a situation?

Nothing. We can't do much in such a situation. All we can do is keep a large enough session timeout to handle small interruptions, but we can't handle total disconnects. Or can we? What about the entire buzz around "Occasionally Connected Computing"?

Occasionally Connected Computing

Occasionally Connected Computing (OCC) is a term coined by Adobe while referring to some of the Rich Internet Applications (RIA). These applications could cache data to the client and function even when the Internet connection was not present. We use the term in the same manner for mobile applications. OCC refers to the kind of software architecture where an application can continue functioning with or without a live Internet connection.

OCC requires a different way of thinking about software architecture. But the ability to run an application without a live connection has tremendous impact on the future of the mobile web. Network connectivity is costly, and users don't like to pay for each byte they download. With the advent of multiple networks, a user might want to do heavy uploads and downloads in a WiFi zone, and only minimal transactions when on GPRS. If our application could provide this flexibility, there are good chances it will be grabbed like sweet candy by the users.

So how can we achieve OCC on mobile devices? While some amount of caching has always been part of mobile applications, OCC is a new thing for the mobile web. As such, OCC is new even for web applications! The OCC poster-boy solution is Google Gears (http://code.google.com/apis/gears/) — a browser extension that provides an API to run applications offline, complete with a caching server, an offline SQL database, and an asynchronous worker pool that lets you do the heavy lifting in the background. Google Gears is certainly an innovation whose time has come.

The following figure shows the architecture of Google Gears (or other OCC models).

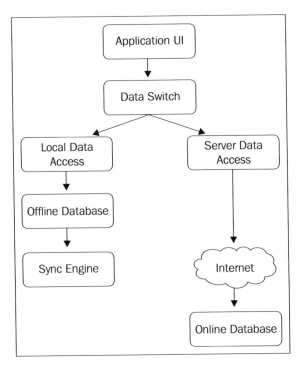

The Dojo Offline Toolkit (`http://dojotoolkit.org/offline`) is a special version of Dojo Toolkit designed for OCC. Dojo Offline is based on Google Gears and provides an easy-to-understand, higher-level access to Gears. It can automatically detect network availability and store data in a lightweight hash table instead of SQL. Dojo SQL allows querying stored data and returns them as easy-to-use JavaScript objects. Dojo is also working on a mobile version of its toolkit, so Dojo Offline is something to watch out for.

If Dojo is using Google Gears, there must be something good about it. The G Company is eyeing the mobile market already and is ready to take it by storm, and it plans to do this with thousands of Androids!

Androids will Invade Your Mobile Space Soon!

Android is the name of Google's mobile operating system and other key software. Google, along with many others, has formed the Open Handset Alliance (www.openhandsetalliance.com)—a group of mobile and technology leaders who want to change the mobile experience for customers. The alliance has released Android SDK, which is an open platform to build applications for mobile devices using Java.

What's so special about Android and the Open Handset Alliance? As such, there have been a number of similar initiatives in the past where groups launched a Linux-based operating system and built tools around it. But there are reasons for Android to be special and why it has the potential to invade our mobile space. Here are a few:

- It is an open-source platform. The license allows commercial use without the need to give back the modifications.

- It treats native and downloaded applications equally. This is unprecedented. It means that if you don't like the phone book application that came with your phone, you can download one that you like and replace it in. You can customize any and everything about the phone—the way you like it.

- Google has taken the native application route rather than the Mobile Web route. You use Java to build applications for the platform. At the same time, there is a capable browser included, and you can easily deploy Mobile Web applications on Android.

- You can also easily integrate various applications on the phone. It's possible (and encouraged) to build applications that use the device capabilities as well as use the Web to get data. You can build an application that uses the location of the device and alerts you when your friends are nearby—right in your phone book!

- Unlike the past efforts, now there is a company with sufficient cash reserves to make this initiative successful! That is a big plus!

- And technologically, the platform has good potential!

The following screenshot shows a sample application running on the Android SDK. If you want to build mobile web applications for Android (`http://code.google.com/android/`), it won't be a big deal. Develop as usual, and just test it with Android SDK. If it works, and most probably it will, you are well set!

Getting Inside the Android

You can use Eclipse to build Android applications and the overall system architecture is quite interesting, especially, the way information is shared between applications. As such, there are four building blocks to an Android application.

- Activities are single-screen UIs. They contain the forms and visual elements, and are implemented as one class per activity. Intents are similar to events, but do a lot more. Moving from one activity (screen) to another is also done via Intents. An IntentFilter decides what Intents an activity can handle.

- IntentReceiver is a way for you to handle external events with your application, for example to invoke your application when a new message arrives or when a contact is edited.

- A Service is like a daemon, running in the background for longer periods.
- Content Providers are data stores. Android comes with SQLite database, but you can use and develop anything that adheres to the Content Provider API.

If you want to know more about Android, the online documentation is a great way to start: `http://code.google.com/android/`. The mailing lists too carry a lot of useful information.

Other Players

While Google and Apple give each other a run for their money, Microsoft is still figuring out what it should do. Microsoft entered the mobile devices market early on and holds a majority of the SmartPhone market. Google and Apple are looking at not only SmartPhones but also standard Feature Phones. Apple has taken a "closed" approach—guarding hardware, software, and even access to device capabilities. Google has gone completely open, giving freedom to do whatever the user/developer wants with the system. The other players—Nokia, Sony, Motorola, etc. have investments in their own software stack, but may join the Google bandwagon in some form or the other. That means Google will have tons of money coming in from advertising on its mobile platform! That is the reason why it's doing all the good work right now, isn't it?

Is the Mobile the Next Computer?

Looking at all the developments in the field and the predictions about proliferation of mobile phones, one may feel that the mobile phone is the next computing device. And that feeling is not far from the truth. A mobile phone is and will be a primary computing device for many consumers. By the numbers, the mobile phone is the most successful consumer device today—ahead of TV and computers. For the majority of consumers, a mobile phone is the most high tech device they own. With the amount of features and processing power cramped into these tiny shells, mobile devices have already become more powerful than computers of a few years ago.

What this means is that there is a huge market to be tapped. The sheer size of the market means a success can take you leaps and bounds. User interaction design is going to be vital for success and a developer must do everything possible to give an easy and smooth experience to the user. It's a challenge to deal with the variety of devices and platforms in the mobile space, but once you have handled the challenge a couple of times, you are equipped to conquer the world!

How will People Use Their Mobile Computer?

If the mobile phone is going to be the computing devices for many, what use are they going to put it to? This will depend on the kind of applications that will come out. But once the basic needs of phone and communication are taken care of, the customers want entertainment and productivity. They want to carry out business tasks on the device or download ringtones and wallpapers. Entertainment keeps an upper hand these days, with millions of dollars transacted every day buying wallpapers, theme, ringtones, and games!

Innovative applications will always find their place. And Mobile Web apps are creating a niche for themselves already. Expect people to use high-end mobile devices as their primary computing devices! Expect people to use all mobile devices as one of their major entertainment devices as well!

Mobile is Not Limited to Phones

We have always maintained that mobile devices are not limited to mobile phones. They will include browsers embedded in automobiles, entertainment devices, and gaming consoles! As a matter of fact, many people are hacking Playstation, Wii, and Xbox and running applications on them. Devices like this are where the real magic of the mobile web starts to appear. Imagine ordering your favorite pizza while you are playing beach volleyball with your friends over neighborhood Wi-Fi. All from the gaming console—just pop open the browser, visit Pizza On The Run, and place your order. Luigi's man will be there within half an hour with delicious pizzas!

And while we are at it, here is some more noteworthy analysis.

Some More Analysis!

We have reviewed the trends and developments in the mobile web and the mobile browsers. Let us look at some other noteworthy analysis and predictions!

Location-Based Services will Mushroom

Increasing numbers of mobile devices are aware of the location now. They can detect the longitude and latitude they are at. This information can then be embedded in a photo taken via geo tags or can be used to retrieve location-based service information. If you are passing by a movie theatre, you may just get a special offer on the movies. Or you can navigate a map through your mobile device itself, without the need to fit a GPS system in your car.

Location-based services like this will mushroom in the coming months. Intelligent use of location information will find user acceptance, the rest will die!

SMS Messaging will Continue Its Hold

More and more service providers realize the benefit of using SMS for notifications and promotions. Mobile networks are full of SMS messages flying around, and this is not going to end. It's becoming easier to integrate SMS-based services—including two-way messaging—and more applications will use SMS in the coming days. Use of MMS will be limited, but SMS will even be used for quizzes, polls, and entertainment.

Mobile Payments will Happen, Albeit Slowly

The mobile commerce and mobile payment industry is still struggling with standards. There are already innovative solutions available—and we saw them in the mobile payments chapter. But it's still some time before mobile payments become mainstream. Person-to-Person and Near-Field communication payments will happen sooner than others. Micro-payments that show up on your bill will have wider acceptance as well.

You will Build Some Kickass Mobile Web Applications

This one is a no brainer. You now know enough to build a mobile web application that integrates with messaging and voice. We have also tried mobile payments and mobile AJAX. You are now equipped to build the next killer mobile web app! All it will take is the focus on users. What works is the application of technology, not the technology itself.

And if you are looking for some additional help, here are are few resources that can support you.

Resources for Mobile Web Integration

Here are a few online resources that will help you keep up to date on mobile web integration:

- W3C's Planet Mobile Web: http://www.w3.org/Mobile/planet, a collection of the most influential blogs on mobile
- dot Mobi's Developer Resources: http://www.dev.mobi

- WAP Tutorials on Developers' Home: `http://www.developershome.com/`
- Openwave Developer Resources: `http://developer.openwave.com/`
- W3C's Mobile Web Initiative: `http://www.w3.org/Mobile/`
- WURFL / WALL etc.: `http://wurfl.sourceforge.net/`

This list is very small, and there are many other sources from which you can learned more about a particular thing in mobile web integration. We have mentioned the links of relevant online resources in each chapter and you should visit them. If you are looking for particular information, doing a quick Google search too will find you good resources!

This is the end of our research on the trends in the mobile web. Let's revise what we did in this chapter!

Summary

This is the last chapter in the book. Over the last ten chapters, we have learned a lot about developing for the mobile web. We learned about XHTML, WCSS, Adaptation, Best Practices, Messaging, Mobile Payment, and Mobile AJAX. This was our take to peek at what lies ahead in the mobile web. We specifically looked at:

- Mobile web applications are growing: every successful web application is being ported to mobile.
- Mobile widgets are the next big thing.
- Mobile browsers are evolving rapidly and will make it easier to develop mobile web applications.
- Mobile networks are complex! And can drop anytime.
- We can implement Occasionally Connected Computing architecture using Google Gears and Dojo Offline.
- Google and Open Handset Alliance are pushing Android.
- SMS and entertainment will continue to dominate.
- For many, mobile devices will be their only computing platform.

There is a big scope for developing innovative mobile web applications. Applications that integrate messaging, voice, payment, and OCC with the Mobile Web have an even greater chance of making it big. The mobile usage will continue to grow for the next few years. Simple ideas that effectively solve a specific problem of mobile users will be very successful—worldwide!

We have submitted our findings to Luigi. He was in deep thought after reading the report. We don't know what will be his next idea, but till that time let's get some pizzas!

Index

Thank you for buying
Mobile Web Development

In the long term, we see ourselves and you—customers and readers of our books—as part of the Open Source ecosystem, providing sustainable revenue for the projects we publish on. Our aim at Packt is to establish publishing royalties as an essential part of the service and support a business model that sustains Open Source.

If you're working with an Open Source project that you would like us to publish on, and subsequently pay royalties to, please get in touch with us.

Writing for Packt

We welcome all inquiries from people who are interested in authoring. Book proposals should be sent to authors@packtpub.com. If your book idea is still at an early stage and you would like to discuss it first before writing a formal book proposal, contact us; one of our commissioning editors will get in touch with you.

We're not just looking for published authors; if you have strong technical skills but no writing experience, our experienced editors can help you develop a writing career, or simply get some additional reward for your expertise.

About Packt Publishing

Packt, pronounced 'packed', published its first book "Mastering phpMyAdmin for Effective MySQL Management" in April 2004 and subsequently continued to specialize in publishing highly focused books on specific technologies and solutions.

Our books and publications share the experiences of your fellow IT professionals in adapting and customizing today's systems, applications, and frameworks. Our solution-based books give you the knowledge and power to customize the software and technologies you're using to get the job done. Packt books are more specific and less general than the IT books you have seen in the past. Our unique business model allows us to bring you more focused information, giving you more of what you need to know, and less of what you don't.

Packt is a modern, yet unique publishing company, which focuses on producing quality, cutting-edge books for communities of developers, administrators, and newbies alike. For more information, please visit our website: www.PacktPub.com.

BlackBerry Enterprise Server for Microsoft® Exchange

ISBN: 978-1-847192-46-2   Paperback: 188 pages

Installation and Administration

1. Understand BlackBerry Enterprise Server architecture

2. Install and configure a BlackBerry Enterprise Server

3. Implement administrative policies for BlackBerry devices

4. Secure and plan for disaster recovery of your server

PHP Web 2.0 Mashup Projects

ISBN: 978-1-847190-88-8   Paperback: 280 pages

Create practical mashups in PHP grabbing and mixing data from Google Maps, Flickr, Amazon, YouTube, MSN Search, Yahoo!, Last.fm, and 411Sync.com

1. Expand your website and applications using mashups

2. Gain a thorough understanding of mashup fundamentals

3. Clear, detailed walk-through of the key PHP mashup building technologies

4. Five fully implemented example mashups with full code

Please check **www.PacktPub.com** for information on our titles

PACKT PUBLISHING

osCommerce Webmaster's Guide to
Selling Online

Increase your sales and profits with expert tips on SEO, marketing, design, selling strategies, etc.

Vadym Gurevych

PACKT

osCommerce Webmaster's Guide to Selling Online

ISBN: 978-1-847192-02-8   Paperback: 400 pages

Increase your sales and profits with expert tips on SEO, Marketing, Design, Selling Strategies, etc.

1. Turn your e-commerce site into a money-making enterprise

2. Full of practical tips and tricks to improve profit with osCommerce

3. Professional advice on choosing the best contributions

Joomla! Cash

Money-making weapons for your Joomla! website

Brandon Dawson   Tom Canavan

PACKT

Joomla! Cash

ISBN: 978-1-847191-40-3   Paperback: 160 pages

Money-making weapons for your Joomla! website

1. Learn to set up a cash-generating Joomla! website

2. Learn to implement a shopping cart on Joomla!

3. How to run an affiliate program from your site

4. Set up streams of income using Joomla!

5. Gain valuable search-engine ranking knowledge

Please check **www.PacktPub.com** for information on our titles